CORYNNE W. PLESS

NEW YORK
INTERIORS

Lannoo

CONTENTS

03

TRIBECA

04

BROOKLYN

05

UPPER WEST & EAST SIDE, QUEENS

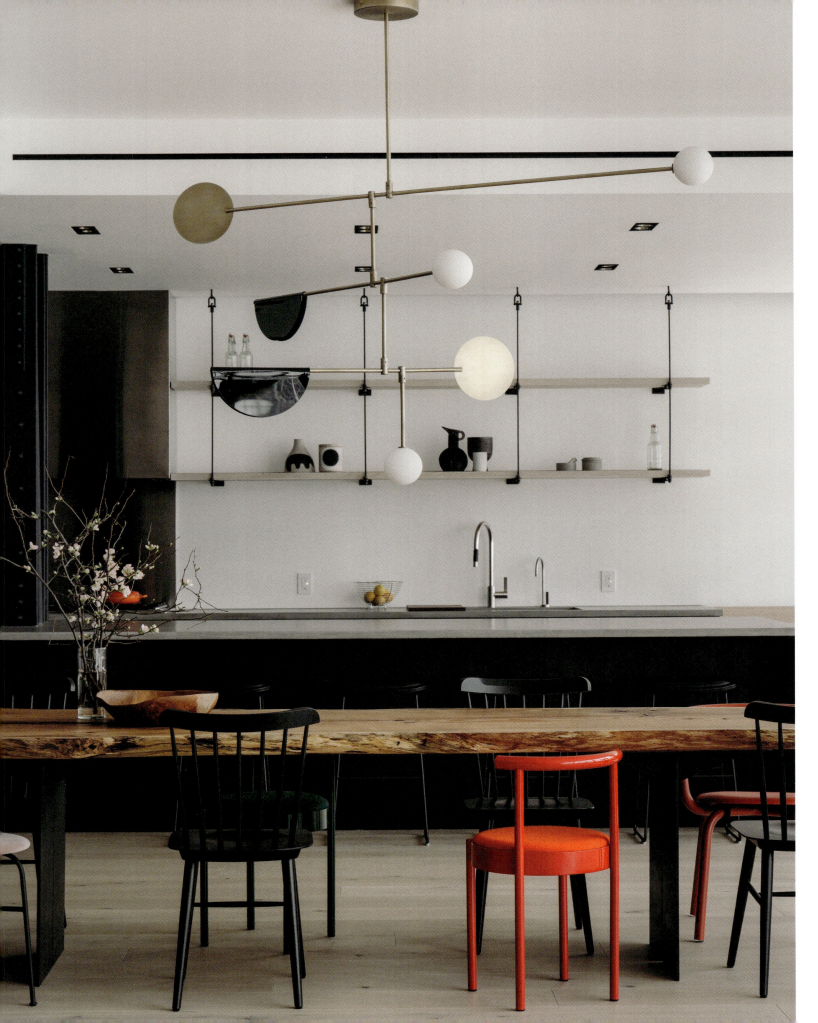

INTRODUCTION

Above New York City's bustling sidewalks, the skyline pulses between the rooftops of centuries-old brownstones, landmark institutions, and soaring skyscrapers, outlining structures from years present and past that define the architectural landscape of America's most populous and rapidly evolving city. Come dusk, this skyline dissolves into a kaleidoscope of twinkling lights, lighting the alleyways and avenues until morning – a passage of time unlike any other. *New York Interiors* highlights the work of up-and-coming and established designers who have carved out their own space in history, in their own time, pioneering New York's design scene into tomorrow.

It's no secret that New York City's abundance of opportunity is gently leveled out by its abundance of constraints. Lack of personal space, natural light, and storage are a few of the many sacrifices required of its residents and guests. Any discomfort, however, can be quickly remedied with a walk in Central Park, a slice of pizza under the Brooklyn Bridge, or the smell of fresh cut flowers outside a corner market. Yet, finding solutions to minimize or enhance the city's limitations is an art of its own. The designers, residents, and architects highlighted in this book creatively reduced the city's sharp and often taxing edge, with innovative solutions that are relatable within any home. In one Tribeca loft, an architecture firm used a very simple mix of organic materials within a bathroom that the client wanted to feel "spa-like" and timeless – many years later, the soothing bathroom stands the test of time and is a welcome reprieve from the city's bustle. Another designer completely revamped a Lower East Side apartment that was lacking in natural light and storage by breaking up a set of small, awkward rooms to form an expansive boudoir. He then designed – and cleverly concealed – a series of closets in the new room, by installing trim-less closet doors with hidden hinges, and coating the doors in the same plaster finish as the walls.

Other enchanting stories, like how New Yorkers, new and old, found and made their way in the city, also fill the pages of this book. You'll discover how a third-generation New York designer transformed a beautiful, yet decaying Brooklyn brownstone to reflect her family's lifestyle, with the help of an attentive architect. A casual friendship between an artist and an interior designer unexpectedly evolved into a partnership (and eventually a new design studio), after the purchase of a house in Queens. And you'll see what happens when an artist decides to plan a party in her historic Tribeca apartment and asks an architect to redesign her house entirely in just six weeks. How the architect relinquished the old and reimagined the new, filling the apartment with a customized menagerie of one-of-a-kind furnishings, color, and elegance was simply amazing, and completed just in time for the pop-and-clink.

The homes featured in *New York Interiors* were gracefully captured by New York-based photographers Nicole Franzen, Nick Glimenakis, Joseph Kramm, Chris Mottalini, and Matthew Williams. And the novel designs and talents brightening every page have made their inimitable mark underneath New York's ever-changing skyline – a beautiful moment, in a beautiful city. Enjoy!

Corynne W. Pless, Los Angeles

LOWER EAST SIDE, NOHO
& EAST VILLAGE
INTERIORS
WEST VILLAGE & CHELSEA
TRIBECA
BROOKLYN
UPPER WEST
& EAST SIDE, QUEENS

01

CHASING THE LIGHT

A creative couple partnered with GRT Architects to transform their century-old apartment into a light-filled, modern-day home.

In a classic turn-of-the-century East Village apartment building, Tal Schori and Rustam Mehta, co-founders of GRT Architects, alongside their team of architects and designers, gently modernized a pre-war apartment into a bright and airy home that gracefully reflects the building's colorful history, as well as their clients' tasteful aesthetics. The corner building, known as Onyx Court, was designed in 1902 by Harde & Short. The lobby, rooms, and corridors feature the era's signature architectural elements such as ornate mosaic work, embellished exterior moldings, unlacquered brass, plastered walls, and parquet flooring. But like many aging New York apartments, the original layout was a bit choppy, and lacked an organic flow or easy access to any natural light. "There was a real sense of being cramped in the space," remembers Schori. "We wanted to totally rethink that in a way that was respectful to the history of the building but appropriate for the way the clients wanted to live in it."

Schori began by chasing the light, finding it framed behind stagnant walls, seen only under doorframes and in the dimly lit hallways. In order to eliminate that onset "cramped" feeling and introduce a natural sense of warmth, the team streamlined the twisting corridor by carving out an uninterrupted path from the entry to the apartment's large, east-facing windows. The revised design includes (and conceals) the laundry room, coat closet, key console, and small bench, all flowing from the entry. At the end of the straight-lined corridor lies the newly placed kitchen – no small feat when working with a co-op – which lies adjacent to the dining and living rooms. The revised layout provides a seamless, free-flowing space between the kitchen, dining, and living rooms – a design perfect for a couple who hosts and entertains often.

Schori then filled the kitchen with a stately, central island dressed in rich oxblood tiles, custom white oak cabinetry paired with oversized wooden pulls, corian white countertops, brass fittings, and a checkerboard floor that trails vertically into a backsplash. These large- and small-scale designs creatively

A textured sliding glass door divides the living room and the office

"There are ways in which we are drawing from things in the building that lead us to these playful reinterpretations or ways of thinking about the history that feel surprising and fun," says Schori.

pay homage to the building's charming architectural features (like the intricate tile work in the lobby and brass sconces found in the apartment), while at the same time providing their clients with a practical design-forward home. "There are ways in which we are drawing from things in the building that lead us to these playful reinterpretations or ways of thinking about the history that feel surprising and fun," adds Schori.

In the living room, the couple's colorful rug inspired the chosen hues that are now cast within the connecting rooms. A warm gray fills the living room walls and an earthy mauve finds a home on the backend of the bookshelf, while a subtle pink stoically covers the shelf's outward-facing panels and includes a sliding central pink panel that conceals a TV screen. Next to the living room, a textured, sliding glass door reveals an intimate office. In the primary suite, which is accessed near the entry, a discreet vestibule leads to the primary bath and bedroom door. "We still tried to maintain this sense that there were separate rooms throughout the house, which is kind of a hallmark of early 20th-century apartment buildings," says Schori.

In the living room, a custom bookshelf designed by GRT Architects conceals a television behind the abstract artwork

"The journey to final product is always one that needs to be delightful and playful, but also surprising to everyone who is involved in the process," says Schori, who with his team (and in collaboration with their creative and ambitious clients) crafted a delightful design that strikes an inviting, new, and historic note throughout.

"We wanted to totally rethink that in a way that was respectful to the history of the building but appropriate for the way the clients wanted to live in it," says Schori.

The kitchen's tiled island is paired with a playfully checkered floor. The custom cabinetry is made of rift-cut white oak wood ← ←

In the living room, a vintage pendant lights the room. The yellow chair (left) is vintage ←

The hallway pendant light is by Anna Karlin ↓

The primary
bedroom is dressed
in a soothing palette
with custom closets
paired with rounded,
wooden handles

Custom millwork designed by GRT Architects defines the desk and allows for additional storage in the bedroom

→

A terrazzo marble
takes over the
primary bathroom
and is adorned with
modern brass
fixtures

A botanical wallpaper is paired with a lush green tile in the powder room

DIVINE DESIGN

Robert Marinelli artfully crafted a new downtown apartment into a comfortable, luxurious home for his client and her daughter.

"She wanted it to have a spirit of its own," says Robert Marinelli of his client, costume designer and fashion consultant Marcee Smith. Marinelli, a bi-coastal designer with a fetching new furniture line and an equally enticing interiors portfolio, worked with Smith on her newly built penthouse in downtown Manhattan, having previously helped design her Upper East Side apartment. That sought-after spirit that Marinelli poetically captured and cast upon every inch of Smith's new 3,500 square foot apartment is authentically luxe, diligently executed, and glistening in a colorful cosmic energy that's truly one of a kind.

For Marinelli, each project starts at the drawing board, where he realizes and problem solves over pen and paper. For Smith's NoHo (North of Houston) apartment, Marinelli began by meshing four bedrooms into three, and carved out a more defined entryway that would double as an intimate art gallery. "Because we had these individual rooms we could create different identities, different feelings, different inspiration in each room," says Marinelli.

He also redesigned the built-in cabinetry and vanities throughout the apartment to accomodate Ms. Smith's specific needs and to convey a more soothing, contemporary aesthetic.

The living area was already divided by a hallway, so Marinelli designated the split room into a formal living space on one side and a casual gathering space on the other. The base moldings here, and in every room, were inverted to give the walls a modernist, floating-like quality. This harmonizes the architectural language throughout the various rooms. The formal living room's wall was clad with unfilled travertine (adhered with steel anchors) and furnished with customized sofas from Marinelli's own furniture collection plus elegant draperies that drop from the ceiling. The traditional fireplace was replaced with an eye-level (when sitting) firebox recessed into the travertine-clad wall. A lacquered writing desk by New Day Woodwork flips into a keyboard – customized for Smith's

In the living room, an artwork by Jack Youngerman, from Irena Hochman Fine Art, hangs next to the 'Cook' swivel chair designed by R. Marinelli Studio

"In New York City apartments, if there's empty or unused spaces, you capture and make them utilitarian and that's what we did here," says Marinelli.

daughter. The more casual family room, which sits opposite the kitchen, opens onto the terrace overlooking the city.

Marinelli redesigned and reconfigured the kitchen cabinetry and layout, beginning with a central island, which hosts a cantilevered concrete bar on top and an abundance of storage below. "In New York City apartments, if there's empty or unused spaces, you capture them and make them utilitarian and that's what we did here," says Marinelli. The dining area hosts an assorted mix of designer furniture from various eras, like the 18th-century carved and painted Italian host and hostess armchairs paired with 1920s chairs by André Sornay. "It is a very eclectic mix but I really like to push the envelope like this when I'm developing the design vocabulary so no two projects look formulaic or the same," says Marinelli. In the home office, Marinelli and Smith had their fun. House of Hackney wallpaper and beaded draperies adorn the color-filled room with eclectic vintage chairs sprinkled in. "It's very whimsical," adds Marinelli.

Conceived in collaboration with art consultant Irena Hochman, the art collection features artworks by Jack Youngerman, Sarah Graham, and Dominic Beattie, among others. In the foyer moonlighting as an art gallery, a series of works by Cy Twombly are framed under a floating constellation. "Rather than do a chandelier, which is what everyone expects, we put a constellation of pin spotlights in the ceiling," says Marinelli. The concave plastered ceiling, custom-made by Hyde Park Moldings and hand-painted by Atelier Premiere, glows from dime-sized star-like holes, which illuminate and romance the cozy enclave.

A custom cement island bar by Oso Industries with barstools by Mondo gently partitions the living room from the kitchen. The glass vase (right) was discovered at Pucci Gallery and the sculptures on the bookshelf are from Cultured Objects

This intricate, yet playful use of materials, textures, and furnishings continues throughout the home, where every room boasts its own warming note to the beat of a glamorous, cosmic melody.

←

A cast aluminum cocktail table by Erwan Boulloud and wing chair covered in Pierre Frey by Hubert Le Gall (from Twenty First Gallery) are surrounded by a pair of 'Cook' swivel chairs, 'Maxime' ottoman, and 'Lara' sofa from R. Marinelli Studio. The side table is by Hervé Van der Straeten and the ceramic sculpture on top is by Peter Lane Clay

→

The custom cabinetry was completed by New Day Woodwork

←

In the entryway turned art gallery, the 'Mushroom' series by Cy Twombly hangs above a 'Red Clay' chair by Maarten Baas from Carpenters Workshop Gallery and a bench by Dimore Studio for the Future Perfect. The plaster walls were created by Atelier Premiere and the multi-color stone flooring was installed by MGO

"We created these special, fun moments throughout the apartment, all of which have different inspirations and personality," says Marinelli.

Wall sconces by Hervé Van der Straeten light the primary bedroom. Art by Sarah Graham from Irena Hochman Fine Art hangs over the '2001' bed from R. Marinelli Studio Collection ←

A custom light sculpture by Éric de Dormael floats above the primary bed. In the bathroom, custom concrete walls and floors were finished by Oso Industries ↓

←←

Wallpaper from House of Hackney, a 1950s Italian desk chair from L'Art de Vivre and the 'Fontana' sofa from R. Marinelli Studio Collection color the home office

←

The 'Goyah' ottoman from R. Marinelli Studio Collection (covered in Edelman leather) sits above a custom round angora area rug woven to match the upholstered wall fabric from Osborne & Little and drapery from Zimmer + Rohde

→

The home office bathroom hosts a vintage 1950s Italian mirror from Bernd Goeckler, custom green lacquer vanity from New Day Woodwork, wallpaper from Elitis, and a framed photograph from Irena Hochman Fine Art

A pair of cast bronze, mask wall sconces by Elizabeth Garouste (from Pucci Gallery) light the onyx floors from BAS Stone, custom cantilevered cast glass sink by John Lewis Glass, and the artwork by Dominic Beattie from Irena Hochman Fine Art

GOING BANANAS

Designer Alex P White transformed a bland apartment on the Lower East Side into a luxuriously wild and highly customized home for his new, dynamic client.

Personalizing a blank canvas requires a bit of magic. For Alex P White, an interior designer with offices in New York and Los Angeles, developing such a magic begins in the books. "You will most often find me buried in a pile of art and design books," says White, who, prior to any design meetings with potential clients, scours magazine and design publications from decades past for inspiration. The idea for a custom bed, influenced by an image of Diane von Furstenberg's master bedroom from a 1980 *Vogue* article titled "A Woman's Domain", had been tucked away by White for just the right client. "My concept was just waiting for the right person to come along that would appreciate the reference and theatrical design," says White, who discovered that client in 2018. "I showed Manuela the reference image and shared my idea. She squealed with delight," remembers White.

His client, Manuela Giannini, is a fashion entrepreneur and founding designer and Chief Creative Director of the lounge wear line, Marietta Baderna. She also developed a luxury clothing rental business, Shop and Share, which operates out of Brazil. "It was very easy to work with Alex, because he knew who I was more than I knew myself," recalls Giannini, who also recounted the numerous kismet moments that fueled the design into its current fiery, exotic state.

Before the project caught air, White was forced to get creative with the apartment's dimly lit, awkward layout. "The weaknesses must become strengths, so I decided to utilize the moody lighting and lack of space as design statements," says White. To reflect more of the light in just the right tone, White coated an opposite wall in a high-gloss black lacquer. He then lined a custom, lime wash plaster bookcase with recessed LED lights, creating more of a "retro-futuristic" statement within the architecture. White also utilized the apartment's existing

An Italian high-back black woven rattan cane chair by Vivai Del Sud sits next to the 'Stone Flower' vase by Magnus Maxine for The Future Perfect

When it came to the prints, textures, and hues, White surprised Giannini with everything she didn't know she wanted.

palette of walnut, black lacquer, and concrete, creatively infusing these materials into his own design concept of "unfurnished", where customized built-in and platform seating, covered in materials and finishes inspired by the apartment's fixed palette, were designed and installed to that end.

When it came to the prints, textures, and hues, White surprised Giannini with everything she didn't know she wanted. During one memorable design meeting, White proposed a wall-to-wall leopard carpet for the primary bedroom, about which Giannini recalled saying, "Alex, are you crazy? I can't do that." But soon, Giannini became obsessed with it. The boudoir's wild carpet was then paired with a custom faux fur bed (inspired by the *Vogue* article), banana print wallcovering, and a cane-paneled pocket door that opens to reveal the rest of the apartment. "Unbeknownst to me, Manuela had a collection of vintage banana print textiles that she was obsessed with and when I showed her the tropical prints designed by costume designer Catherine Martin there was no question I had landed on something special," says White. Additionally, the boudoir conceals an ample amount of storage (a must for anyone in fashion), which White made disappear like a vanishing act, by installing trim-less doors and concealed hinges within the recessed closets.

In addition to the ultra-customized and colorful furnishings, White placed a few iconic vintage pieces with a selection of contemporary designs in an effort to provoke a more historical and interesting dialogue within. "Stylistically, I think we created a moody, atmospheric oasis that is retro-futuristic-noir meets 1930s Moderne with a touch of 1980s music video vibe that, to me, still feels *au courant*," says White. And for Giannini, the apartment became her dream home and "an extension of my soul."

The 'Serpienta Abaca' rug by Charles Hyman & Herrera for Patterson Flynn glides through the living space. The center table, 'Nero Marquina', was designed by Alex P White

"It was very easy to work with Alex, because he knew who I was more than I knew myself," says Giannini.

The custom built-in platform sofa was finished in tadelakt ← ←
plaster with loose cushions in anti-pilling, stain-resistant
Mokum 'Zebre' fabric

Another Italian high-back black woven rattan cane chair ←
by Vivai Del Sud sits under the custom desk, designed by
Alex P White

A custom cane-clad pocket door, designed by Alex P ↓
White, was fabricated by Wild Willy's Woodshop

→

The custom bed was
designed by Alex P
White, and the
wallpaper is 'Le
Palma' by Catherine
Martin for Mokum

The wall-to-wall leopard flooring is 'Wildcat' by Stark Carpet

02

EAST TO WEST

In just eleven months, interior designer Francis Toumbakaris transformed a historic West Village townhouse into a luxurious haven for his West Coast client.

When one of Francis Toumbakaris' clients called with the news that she had found the most amazing house, he wasn't quite expecting the next line. "I, one hundred percent, non-negotiable, want our living room to be a speakeasy bar." Toumbakaris, a high-end New York-based interior designer, wasn't completely surprised by the idea – his client is a lively media executive from California with a sophisticated and colorful palette. The designer admits that this type of call doesn't happen every day, or for some, ever. "This is so a-typical, what she asks from me," says Toumbakaris, noting that the other way around (designers pushing wild ideas onto the client) is more common. "I say to the universe: more of this please," says Toumbakaris.

The client moved to New York in 2018, but her dream of living in a West Village townhouse only came true a few years later. "The West Village is the most charming neighborhood in all of New York, if not the world," says the owner. "I love the character of the houses, the neighborhood

restaurants and bars, everyone knows each other – it literally is a village."

The client and Toumbakaris came up with a simple narrative, one that would feel engaging, surprising, personal, and historic, with a splash of modernity. "Francis and I have worked together multiple times already," says the client, "so this project was really figuring out how we were going to need to live and work in the space and layout, and designing each floor accordingly." Toumbakaris delights in the process of placement, flow, and storytelling, something he credits to his former days as a ballet dancer. "Before I start decorating a space, I first choreograph a space," says Toumbakaris, who delicately, yet rigorously, perfected each room's layout before he dabbled in the details.

Beginning on the first floor, a marble fireplace, black oak cabinets, aging brass, a custom dining banquet, and a decadent

A marble fireplace mantle, made with bespoke stone by Material Bespoke Stone & Tile (Donna Mondi Collection), is surrounded by the gorgeous 'Namban' wallcovering by De Gournay. The custom dining table was designed by Lucas Leibman in collaboration with Francis Toumbakaris, while the chairs by Costantini Pietro are covered in Elitis fabric

The client and Toumbakaris
came up with a simple narrative,
one that would feel engaging,
surprising, personal, and historic,
with a splash of modernity.

wall covering produce a stately first impression that define the kitchen and dining room. The stairwell, which was original to the home, was preserved, providing access to the remaining four floors. Moving up, the living room, where the speakeasy resides, fills the second floor. Toumbakaris customized every inch of the living room to transport guests into another era, pulling his inspiration from a Gucci chair that the client came across in a department store. The ceiling was finished in a gilded patina, all architectural elements were enhanced and handmade by artists, antique lighting was installed throughout, and nearly every edge is discreetly fringed, like the tassels on a flapper dress in the Prohibition era. "'The speakeasy is better than any New York City bar' – that's a direct quote from multiple people who have been there," says the owner. "It's the quintessential entertaining room," she adds. The bar's millwork, designed by Toumbakaris and produced in house, exudes the same "masculine feel with feminine accents" seen and felt throughout the second floor.

On the third floor, the owner's office checks all the boxes— it's fun, feminine, theatrical, a hint of the 1960s, functional (there's a coffee bar and mini-fridge hidden in the custom millwork), and simply luxe. "Every person that walks in the office says 'this looks like you'," says the owner. "He nailed it." The primary bedroom and bathroom, located on the fourth floor, were designed in a more calm, neutral tone. Originally, the fifth floor was designated to act as a more transitional space or perhaps just an extra floor for storage, but when the owner's partner suggested the idea of a media room in the likeness of a yacht... "I grabbed that idea and went to town," remembers Toumbakaris. Custom mahogany millwork, warm lighting, and a framed painting of the sea are a few of the many nautical nods throughout that Toumbakaris applied to the media room. "It is a magical house," says the owner.

The countertop is in Calacatta Vagli from New York Stone, the kitchen cabinets are embellished with Armac Martin hardware, and the metal shelving is by Amuneal. The pendant lighting in the dining room is from Apparatus

◄ ◄ ◄

In the living room, a portrait of Robert De Niro (right) by Richard Corman is hung over a custom banquette designed by Francis Toumbakaris, upholstered in 'Regale' by Scalamandré. An antique chandelier from High Style Deco lights a settee and swivel chair by Vittoria Frigerio, with wallcoverings from Phillip Jeffries adding a delicate texture throughout

◄ ◄

The speakeasy bar was designed by Francis Toumbakaris and equipped with custom 'Fluted' barstools from Artistic Frame and hardware from Rocky Mountain Hardware. The beautiful hand-painted ceiling was completed by L'Avventura

◄

Authentic 1920s sconces from HighStyle Deco light the living room. The mirror (from Skyframe) conceals a television over the custom fireplace made with bespoke stone by Material Bespoke Stone & Tile (Donna Mondi Collection)

➜

A framed photograph by Slim Aarons is on display over a plush sofa bed from Milano Smart upholstered in Alessandro velvet. The tropical 'Martinique Grasscloth' wallcovering adds a playful narrative in the office corner

A ceiling light, made of Murano glass and discovered on 1stDibs, lights the office, where a desk chair from Brickfield Furniture Co, upholstered in Kravet's 'Clarke and Clarke' fabric, a custom rug designed by Francis Toumbakaris in collaboration with Nourison, and a stately desk, customized by Toumbakaris, playfully convene. A painting by Alberto Murillo is centered over a custom fireplace made with bespoke stone by Material Bespoke Stone & Tile (Donna Mondi Collection)

→

Antique sconces
(from Carlos
Antiques) and an
antique pendant
(from Olde Good
Things) light the
powder room. The
circular, fluted sink
is from Country
Floors and the
copper wallcover
(made with
authentic US
pennies) is from
Indy Penny Tile

The primary bedroom is clad in chic 'The Grove' wallcovering by Phillip Jeffries. The ceiling light is from Hudson Valley Lighting and the bed was sourced from Room & Board and upholstered in 'Luxe Grid' from Holly Hunt

→

A beautiful Sean Lavin pendant from Visual Comfort lights the colorful bathroom. The vanity is from Lacava

Custom millwork, a
Ralph Lauren for
Visual Comfort
chandelier, 'Tatiana'
coffee table from
Arteriors, and a rug
by Christopher Guy
for Nourison bring
warmth and comfort
into this nautical
themed room on the
fifth floor

IN THE WAKE OF LEGACY

David Alhadeff thoughtfully brings The Future Perfect's contemporary design pieces into an iconic brownstone in the West Village, last remodeled by acclaimed architect David Chipperfield.

Finding the perfect home takes time. "We wanted something atypical, something that stood apart from the standard," says David Alhadeff, founder of design platform The Future Perfect. His three-year search abruptly ended after touring a 19th-century, five-story townhouse nestled on a landmarked street in the West Village. Its interiors were remodeled in the late 1990s by leading architect David Chipperfield, and this quintessential New York townhouse reimagined by a master architect naturally became the perfect pied-à-terre for Alhadeff, whose concept of home similarly stands apart from the rest.

Alhadeff spends most of his time in Los Angeles, where he lives with his husband Jason Duzansky and their son, in a newly renovated 1916 Hollywood estate. The estate, like their New York pied-à-terre, is also home to The Future Perfect, Alhadeff's celebrated art and design residential gallery that exhibits emerging and established artists and designers throughout the year and within his home. This

idea of a residential gallery started in 2017, after Alhadeff began placing the gallery's original works of art, limited-edition pieces, and one-of-a-kind furnishings into his own architecturally considered homes, then welcoming his friends, clients, and anyone else inclined to experience them. "There's a broader highway now to fit the definition of gallery programming environment," says Alhadeff.

When Alhadeff received the keys to his East Coast haven, there was little to be done apart from moving in. "We had to change nothing," says Alhadeff. "It was perfect." The front door opens into the parlor, where 12-foot ceilings complement Chipperfield's elegant and stately design. "It's very pristine and it's minimalist to that extent, it's very Chipperfield," says Alhadeff. In the center of the home is a sculptural staircase commanding its way through each floor, beginning in the subterranean kitchen. Going up from the kitchen, the

The 'Palm' mirror by Bower Studios hangs next to the 'Daisy' table by Chris Wolston, 'Melt' lounge chair (also by Bower Studios) and a vintage tuareg rug. The 'Yarumo' wall sconce by Chris Wolston and the 'Marenco' sofa by Arflex are reflected in the mirror

"We wanted something atypical, something that stood apart from the standard," says David Alhadeff.

garden floor, where Alhadeff and company find themselves most often, is warmed by a grand fireplace, with low ceilings amplifying the coziness and louvered doors opening to a lush garden. On the third floor, which hosts the parlor and entry, Alhadeff has arranged his unique collection of designer furnishings and works of art to compose a living room and dining room throughout the open layout, while the upper two floors host the sleeping quarters.

The Future Perfect's New York outpost showcases works by a variety of artists working in diverse disciplines and media, with exhibitions interchanging every six to eight weeks on all floors. "We work with a lot of established artists and designers at this point, but I have a passion for emerging talent," says Alhadeff, who has recently exhibited pieces by Alana Burns, Guy Corriero, Piet Hein Eek, John Hogan, Floris Wubben, and Rahee Yoon, among many others. Crafting this overlap between work and play and the contemporary and historic has just begun for Alhadeff: "I want to continue to play in this medium. For me personally it is very exciting."

The 'Flora' chandelier, by In Common With, is suspended over a glazed, ceramic table, 'Wave Table – Paris Balcony' by Studio Floris Wubben. The lamp, designed by Sophie Lou Jacobsen for In Common With, sits above the 'Whale' bench from Studio Floris Wubben. The wooden cupboards are from Piet Hein Eek and the rug is 'Paysage' from Atelier Février. The 'Throne' chair (left) is also by Floris Wubben

The Future Perfect's New York outpost showcases works by a variety of artists working in diverse disciplines and media.

A stunning fixture by Bocci lights the 'Orion Table with Metal Sleeve' by De La Espada. The velvet 'Cursa' lounge chair, walnut 'Deneb' chair, and 'Deneb' desk are by De La Espada. The 'Geotransition' mirror is from Chen Chen & Kai Williams, vessels are 'Fungus Vases' by David Valner and the stone sculptures are by Ian Collings ← ←

The 'Sela' dining chair and 'Twenty-Five' desk from De La Espada bring a warmth into the corner. The 'Candle' floor lamp and 'Fiber' pendant are from Blue Green Works. The 'Collage' rug is by Atelier Février ←

Vases by David Valner are on display above the 'Arts and Crafts' cabinet by De La Espada. The 'Geotransition' mirror is from Chen Chen & Kai Williams and hangs over wallpaper by Calico ↓

←

A comfortable collection of sofa and chairs, part of the 'Cousy Sofa' collection from Arflex, adorn the parlor floor. The 'Tropical' chandelier by Chris Wolston is suspended over the 'La Ville' rug from Atelier Février, with the aluminum 'Madonna' coffee table (also by Chris Wolston), and a sculptural 'Halo' lamp from Bradley Bowers

→

A colorful rug from Atelier Février is tucked under the 'Tasmi' chair by Chris Wolston, 'Blowing' stool by Seungjin Yang, the 'Drape' desk by De La Espada, and the 'Earthly Delight' vessel by Chris Wolston. The 'Mobile Chandelier 11' is by Michael Anastassiades

The rug
'Transparencia' is by
Atelier Février &
The Future Perfect,
the chandelier is by
Bocci, and the
'Fungus' vase by
David Valner. The
'Albireo' sofa,
'Twenty-Five
Bergère' chair, and
'Twenty-Five
Medium' coffee
table are by De La
Espada

NEW BEGINNINGS

An art-enthused client asked interior designer Julia Blanchard to fill her new home, in a new neighborhood, with a brand-new aesthetic.

"It was all about the views," says Julia Blanchard, a New York-based interior designer, of her longtime client's West Village home. The apartment was located within a mixed-use building designed by Selldorf Architects, a practice founded by the renowned architect Annabelle Selldorf. The three-bedroom apartment was drenched in light with views of Manhattan's picturesque skyline framed throughout. "When I found this apartment, it just had so much light and brightness to it that it just felt like the right place to be," recalls the owner, who was moving downtown from the Upper East Side. Blanchard and her client are well-versed in each other's tastes, skills, and comfort levels, having previously worked together on several of the client's residential projects. But this time, the client wanted a design that was completely new, something different but that still felt like home. "We started from scratch in many ways," says the client.

Blanchard happily accepted the challenge. "It's like taking everything that someone has gravitated towards, and trying to change it," she says. Blanchard, who launched her design firm, Blanchard Design, in 2016, credits her eclectic, yet sophisticated design approach to her art school education and bi-coastal upbringing, meaning Boston and Paris. "I'm very European. I grew up in households where you have Roche Bobois married with Ikea," says Blanchard, who delights in the high/low, "no rules" design approach to making a home.

For her client's freshly built downtown apartment, Blanchard began anew, working alongside the pre-existing deck of tones and materials first envisioned by Selldorf Architects. The designer hung a chandelier by Allied Maker to delicately light the kitchen table and the framed work on paper by artist Donise English. In the dining room a large B&B Italia dining table is placed under a Roll & Hill chandelier. "I wanted to have something playful that also ties into the artwork," says Blanchard, who left plenty of wall

A framed work of art by Devan Shimoyama brightens the view overlooking Manhattan. The floor lamp is from Love House and the stool is from Studio Van Den Akker

"I love to do lighting that is also sculptural and artistic in a way and isn't so contrived," says Blanchard.

space for her client, who is a budding art collector and on the board of trustees for one of the city's largest art museums.

In the living room, Blanchard customized a built-in storage unit, a practical necessity, but designed the unit to display works of art (where currently a Basquiat print the owner purchased over twenty years ago is exhibited), conceal storage, and shelve her client's growing collection of literature and artbooks. The sculptural winged chairs, covered in a poppy cool blue, were placed so your eye travels back into the room, which is lit through an array of circular wall sconces. "I love to do lighting that is also sculptural and artistic in a way and isn't so contrived," says Blanchard.

The primary bedroom had to feel peaceful and calm for her client. Blanchard kept the tone subdued, yet feminine by bringing new and vintage furnishings into the mix. The guest room was curated to be "your quintessential pied-à-terre guest bedroom," says Blanchard. A bed designed by Kelly Wearstler for Lulu and Georgia welcomes guests with impeccable views of Manhattan through the windows. In the office, Blanchard hired an artist to hand-paint a wallpaper-inspired design in a gold-leaf technique on every wall in the room. "It's busy and visual, but it's a very somber room," says Blanchard.

"This space, every aspect of it is pretty welcoming and comfortable," says the owner, who watches over the city from every corner in the warmth of her new home. "I feel very fortunate."

A work by Donise English hangs on the wall next to the kitchen counter. The room is lit by pendants from Allied Maker, while the 'Mathilda' bar stools are by Patricia Urquiola for Moroso

"Every aspect of this space is pretty welcoming and comfortable," says the owner, who watches over the city from every corner in the warmth of her new home. "I feel very fortunate."

In the living room, the millwork was produced by HLP Construction. The art light is from Visual Comfort and the sconces are from Allied Maker. The daybed is from Love House, chairs from B&B Italia, and the coffee table, side table, and sofa are from M2L ← ←

A sculptural chandelier from Roll & Hill lights the table and chairs from B&B Italia ←

The hallway is dressed in a wallcovering from Casamance, rug from Sunshine Thacker, and ceiling flush mount designed by Kelly Wearstler. The 'Le Seat' pouf is by Sunshine Thacker ↓

→

Blanchard worked
with the existing
primary bathroom
design, adding a few
textures and fabrics
to soften the feel

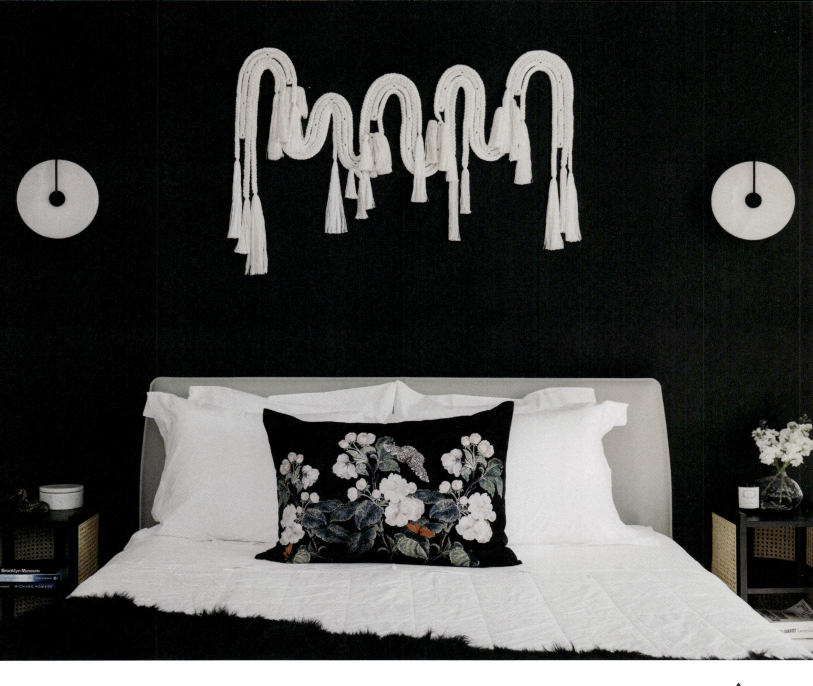

The elegant primary
bedroom keeps a
simple black, white,
and floral palette.
The 'Vella' bed is
from Design Within
Reach, sconces from
Allied Maker, and
the artwork over the
bed is by Karen
Gayle Tinney

CHELSEA DREAMING

A young couple with an impeccable art collection tapped interior designer Tali Roth to help transform their dated townhouse into the perfect family home.

A rip-up-ready, three-bedroom duplex on a tree-lined street in Chelsea checked all the boxes for Paige and Benjamin Zachs. "We had been living in Chelsea for many years, so had really fallen in love with the neighborhood," says Paige, who hunted down malleable-only properties so they could customize the home to their liking. Soon, their lucky real estate find appeared. It came with south-facing windows, a bedroom in the back (so it's nice and quiet) and was located within a beautiful brownstone building on an idyllic tree-lined street – check, check, check.

Soon after the couple purchased their home, they met with Tali Roth of Studio Tali Roth. "We hit it off immediately. They felt so familiar to me," remembers Roth, who splits her time between her two studios in Melbourne, Australia and New York City. Benjamin, a business owner of Fine Fettle, and Paige, an executive at Coterie, put together a lengthy deck of reference images for Roth to pull from, but ultimately gave Roth the reigns to design anew. "I could see

so much potential in the space and the ideas were flowing," says Roth. Roth took their desire for a clean, neutral aesthetic within a visually encaptivating environment to the drawing board and created a vibrant, yet serene home for the couple to comfortably enjoy with their new son.

Like in many brownstones, Roth began with a layout that was narrow and a bit complicated. To combat that immediate cramped feeling, Roth opened up the walls surrounding the kitchen and dining room, a move that provided the couple with an extra workspace and room for an elongated dining table with plenty of seats to host large gatherings – a favorite pastime of theirs. "The layout alone was probably one of the more innovative solutions," says Paige. Roth then brought in neutral tones, calm textures, and elegant finishes to the two social spaces and carried a refined minimalist aesthetic thoughtfully into the rest of the home.

Colorful cushions and throws brighten the custom sofa from Zev. The vase is by contemporary Italian glass artist Pino Signoretto

"We had been living in Chelsea for many years, so had really fallen in love with the neighborhood," says Paige.

In the closetless primary bedroom, Roth designed a three-quarter wall, placing the bed on one side and a string of custom wooden closets on the other. "It makes the space much more chic and adds in way more storage," says Roth. Three types of marble, Roman beige travertine, Verde Alpi green marble, and Paonazzo marble, were boldly, yet modestly used in the bathrooms and kitchen, bringing a more organic and earthy vibe into the monochromatic narrative.

In the living room, an Annie Morris stack sculpture takes center stage. "We bought this work to commemorate the birth of our first son, Louis, with the idea that we will pass this on to him when he gets married, has kids, or goes through a pivotal life moment," says Paige. Ben and Paige began collecting art when they first married nearly ten years ago, a hobby influenced by Ben's grandparents, from whom they inherited a large-scale Chuck Close piece and a work by Kevin Harman. Ben and Paige have since added works by Pino Signoretto, Chase Hall, and Taylor Hays to their growing collection. "I'm a minimalist and love art you can take with you everywhere," says Paige.

In the kitchen, a custom wooden table seats up to ten guests. The marble backsplash is paired with a plastered, fluted wall, light wooden cabinetry, and state-of-the-art appliances

"I'm a minimalist and love art you can take with you everywhere," says Paige.

The 'Concho' coffee table (from The Future Perfect), 'Sesann' lounge chair by Gianfranco Frattini for Cassina, and 'Milano' strip rug from Roth's own bespoke collaboration collection at Empire Rugs Collection fill the living room, where an Annie Morris stack sculpture takes center stage

Naturally hued variegated marble from BAS Stone adds an earthy tone to the minimalistic kitchen

A simple mix of wood and stone fill the elegant bathroom

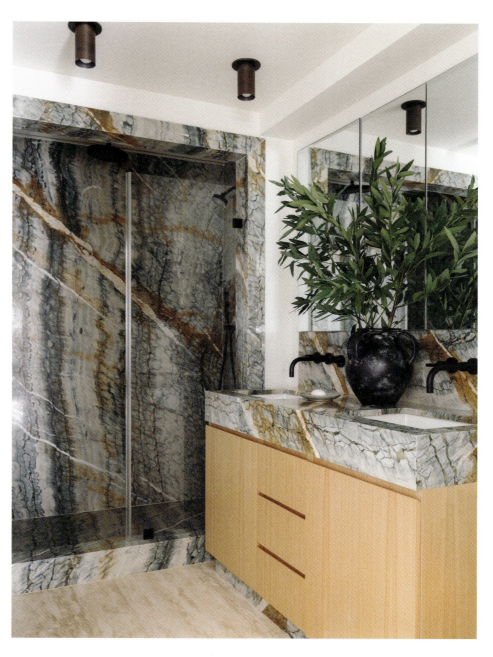

←←

In the living room, a large frosted 'Murano' chandelier lights the eclectic mix of furnishings, new and old. The colorful stacked sculpture is by Annie Morris

←

'Paonazzo' marble from BAS Stone was used for the kitchen countertops and backsplash

→

A painting by Chuck Close (left), nightstands from Anthropologie, cozy linens, and a rug from Armadillo delicately personalize the primary bedroom

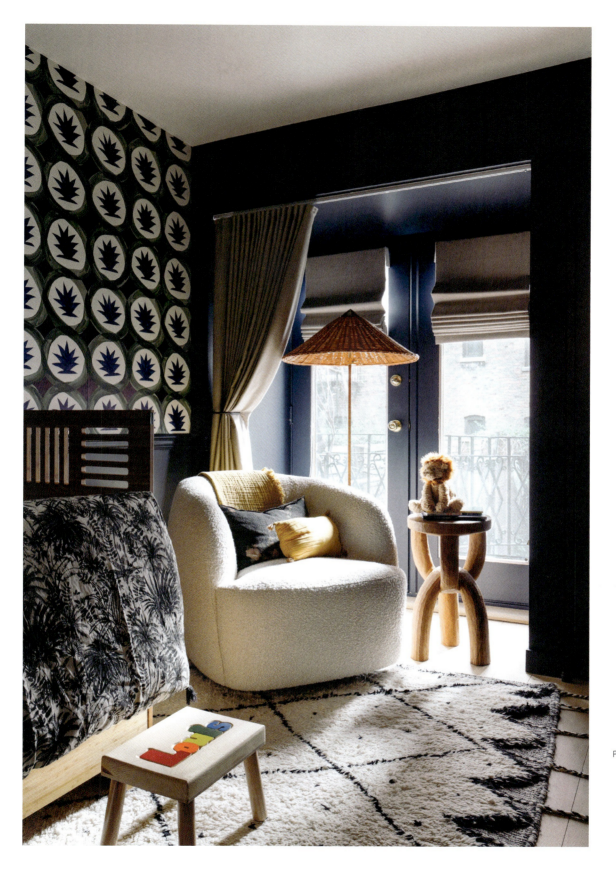

Bold and colorful textiles and furnishings fill the playful nursery. The rug is from Etsy, the armchair was sourced at CB2, and the crib is from Kalon

A CHELSEA STORY

Kristina O'Neal and Adam Gordon redesigned their two-story apartment in Chelsea to reflect the couple's evolving lifestyles and impeccable collection of art, furniture, and everything in between.

In 2023, when Adam Gordon and Kristina O'Neal realized their home of seven years could use a little reshaping, they redesigned their two-story home to better respond to the evolution of their family and growing art collection. "For me, design has a responsibility to respond to the needs of those who inhabit it – what they need at that particular moment, or even what they don't realize they need until they feel it," says O'Neal, a founding partner at the international multidisciplinary hospitality firm, AvroKO. The home, a 3,300 square foot apartment in West Chelsea, was also the brain child of Gordon, who partnered with Steven Harris of Steven Harris Architects and the real estate investment firm Tavros to see it through. When Gordon imagined the apartment and its future residents, he had one client in mind: "Kristina and I. We wanted something for our creative family – a place where we could live with art and treasures we've collected over time."

The seven-month renovation began in the primary suite, where the couple expanded the bedroom into the library. The small stretch into an adjoining room "enabled us to live with more of our art and design," says Gordon. "Art has always been a central character in our lives." The couple also moved the kitchen upstairs, closer to the terrace, where they began finding themselves more often than not. "The terrace is this wonderful liminal space – both connected to the pulse of the city and removed from it, almost like a private oasis," says O'Neal. In the new vacancy downstairs, Gordon and O'Neal added two more suites for when their sons come to visit.

Within the apartment's open, yet defined layout, gallery-like walls and floor-to-ceiling windows are sprinkled throughout. On the walls, Gordon and O'Neal display their collection of fine art, which for Gordon began

On the terrace, the bas-relief work on the wall is by Frédéric Texier, while the sculpture (right) is by an unknown artist

"Kristina and I. We wanted something for our creative family – a place where we could live with art and treasures we've collected over time," says Gordon.

with a collection of midwestern Amish quilts, and eventually melded into its current co-authored state of works by Picasso and Donald Baechler, among many others. "Our collection is a mix – works by established artists and emerging voices, each bringing something unique," says Gordon. "Any art that celebrates the colorful and awkward gets my full attention," adds O'Neal. The collection for both creatives is about connection and the stories and memories embedded in each work that narrate their own journey.

On each floor, the couple displays their love for authentically crafted furniture. "Our furniture reflects our appreciation for pieces that feel grounded, soulful, and made with intention," says O'Neal. The couple has long admired (and diligently hunted down) the craftsmanship produced by Brazilian modernist designers, such as Sergio Rodrigues and Joaquim Tenreiro. "There's a warmth and timelessness to their work that resonates with us," says Gordon. The "soft modernity", yet approachable designs produced by the South American designers evoke a soulful warmth that the couple finds endearing.

The framed works of art (top left and bottom right) are by Andrew Zuckerman, the artwork (top right) is by Donald Baechler, while the sculptural work of art (hung, bottom right) is by Frédéric Texier. Four 'Tulip' chairs, by Pierre Paulin for Artifort, surround a table designed by Boffi De Padova

This highly personalized and inspiring home is a beautiful reflection of two shapeshifting creatives who have kept New York, art, and design at the heart of it all.

"Our furniture reflects
our appreciation for pieces
that feel grounded, soulful,
and made with intention,"
says O'Neal.

In the living room, a sofa by Vladimir Kagan is paired
with a 'Petalas' coffee table by Jorge Zalszupin, lounge
chairs by Móveis Cimo, and a 'Dinamarquesa' armchair by
Jorge Zalszupin by Etel. The artwork (left) is by
Donald Baechler

A wood and resin side table by Andrianna Sharmaris sits
next to the 'Dinamarquesa' armchair. The sculpture is
by Frédéric Texier and the artwork by Donald Baechler

In the kitchen, a Marie Michielssen vase sits on
the Calacatta Quartzite countertop

← ←

An artwork by Matt
Morris is hung over
the primary bed.
The life-sized sheep
sculpture is from
Clic and the 'Elsie'
pendant is by Mitzi
from Hudson Valley
Lighting. In the
corner, a marble
bistro table is paired
with Carlo Scarpa
walnut dining chairs

←

A portrait by Pablo
Picasso hangs above
an aluminum console
table by Bixby.
The 1970s Italian
rocking chair sits
next to a table by
Jacques Poussine

→

The guest room
hosts an impeccable
collection of
furnishings and fine
art. The colorful
portrait, by Pablo
Picasso, is on display
above a desk by Paul
McCobb and walnut
chair by Carlo
Scarpa. The small
stool is by Christian
Siriano and the
corner chair was a
custom design

Two works of art
by Donald Baechler
are exhibited in the
guest bedroom.
A pair of Frédéric
Texier lamps and
a 'Jadssox Silk'
pendant light
the room

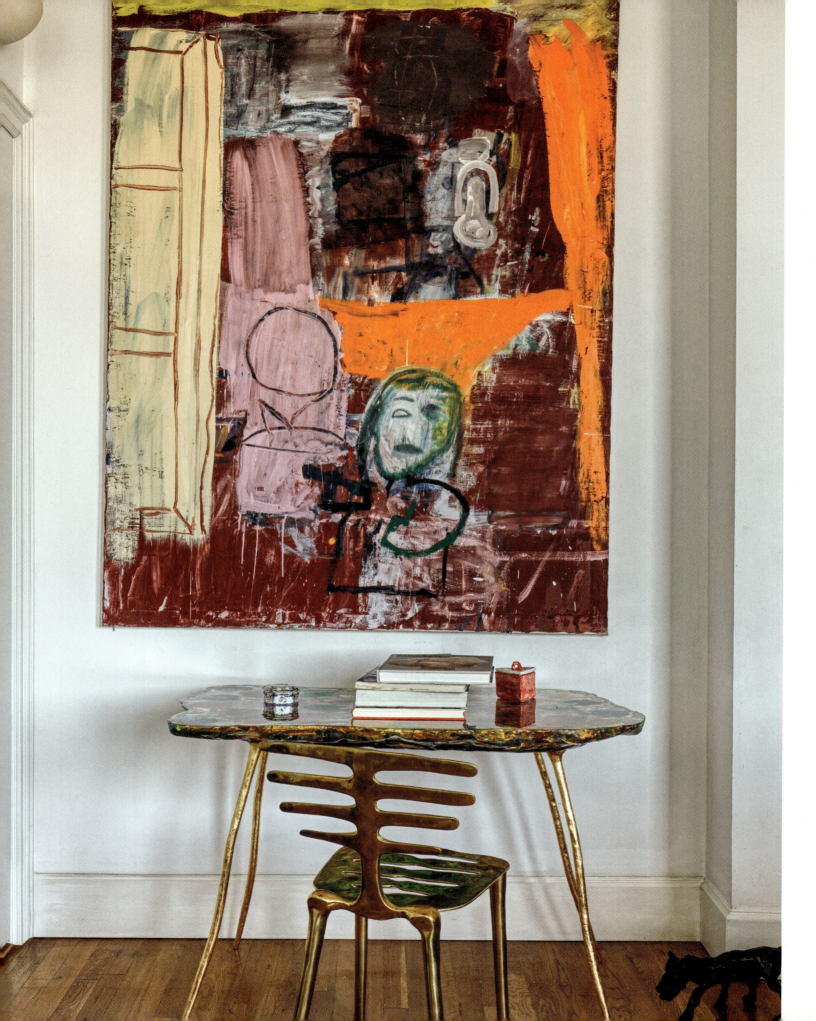

03

TWO OF A KIND

A pair of empty nesters called upon designers Jayne and Joan Michaels to transform a beloved bachelor pad into a cozy pied-à-terre.

Nestled in one of Tribeca's turn-of-the-century landmark buildings, a loft with a stirring past was recently redesigned into an elegant pied-à-terre – a dream made true by Jayne and Joan Michaels of design studio 2Michaels for their long waiting clients. "It only took 35 years to figure it out," laughs the husband, a financier who purchased the property in the mid-1980s. The spacious two-bedroom loft hosts 13-foot-high ceilings and started out as the owner's coveted bachelor pad. When he lived there, he listened to other seasoned tenants share stories about his loft's glory days as a movie set, rehearsal stage, and a dark room. "For the time, it was a very interesting and fun place to live," recalls the owner, who would also occasionally meet Robert De Niro or Harvey Keitel in the hallways.

The young bachelor eventually married and left New York to raise his family and decided to keep the apartment, leasing it to various tenants over the years including De Niro, who briefly made it his personal gym. When the loft wasn't occupied, the couple and their kids would swoop into the empty apartment with air mattresses, sleeping bags, and rollerblades to enjoy a brief New York weekend. The couple always dreamed of returning to the loft, but knew they needed to redesign the layout to better accommodate their family. The husband hired architect after architect who attempted to personalize the space, add a second bedroom, more storage, etc. but the design was never quite right. "It was always the box in the box," says the husband. Year after year, actually decade after decade, the underwhelmed couple shelved the latest architectural renderings and slowly continued their search for the perfect design.

Shortly after the couple became empty nesters, the husband once again reignited his search for a designer, stumbling across the website of Jayne and Joan Michaels – twin sisters based in New York with a knack for creating elegant, personalized spaces for their clients. After their first site visit to the loft, Jayne and

In the entry, a vintage mirror from 1stDibs hangs above custom console from Crump & Kwash

Jayne and Joan creatively divided each space through subtle furnishing arrangements, which kept the design open, yet defined.

Joan called upon their friend and architectural designer, Jeffrey English. English quickly sketched the loft's "eureka" plan. "It sounds simple, because it's just an open box, but no one else really thought it through and figured out a way to actually create what they created," says the husband.

To start, Jayne and Joan researched industrial lofts and materials from the 19th century, then creatively curated their findings into the apartment's elevated redesign. "We were drawn to geometric shapes and circles," says Joan, who paired the linear pieces with neutral and organic textures and tones. The building's original architectural elements, like the wooden floors, open layout, and oversized windows, were left alone, while the crown moldings and baseboards were reconditioned. The dusty billiard table, exercise equipment, and leather sofas were replaced with custom furnishings, Swedish pottery, a stately glass chandelier, and an impeccable custom rug by Judy Ross (in collaboration with Jayne and Joan). "When you're in the space, the rug really enhances it without taking over," says Jayne. The Michaels creatively divided each space through subtle furnishing arrangements, which kept the design open, yet defined. The dining room comfortably hosts large gatherings, while the living room offers multiple places to relax, read, and make a drink (from the bar hidden behind the bookshelf's sliding doors). The owners' personal belongings, like their inherited collection of Walt Whitman books and objects, a desirous record collection, World War Two hardbacks, and a series of theater photographs by Hiroshi Sugimoto, all bring in a heartwarming tone. "It was sort of always my dream to leave New York, raise a family, then come back some day," says the wife, who now hosts holidays and family gatherings around their extended dining room table overlooking lower Manhattan. "It's got the biggest place in our hearts."

A pair of Swedish armchairs from Wyeth, an ottoman from Lawson-Fenning, and a custom chaise lounge from Interiors by George & Martha mingle above a rug designed by 2Michaels in collaboration with Judy Ross

"It was sort of always my dream to leave New York, raise a family, then come back some day," says the wife, who now hosts holidays and family gatherings around their extended dining room table overlooking lower Manhattan.

A series of photographs, titled 'Theater', by Hiroshi Sugimoto are on display in the dining room. The table is custom Douglas fir by Rob Pluhowski and accompanied by 'Plank' chairs by Roland Rainer ← ←

The kitchen hosts a custom island and cabinetry designed by Jeffrey English and 2Michaels. Three 'Line Wall' lights by Snelling light the room ←

The sculpture 'Tower' by James Beardan is on display under the custom staircase leading to the primary bedroom ↓

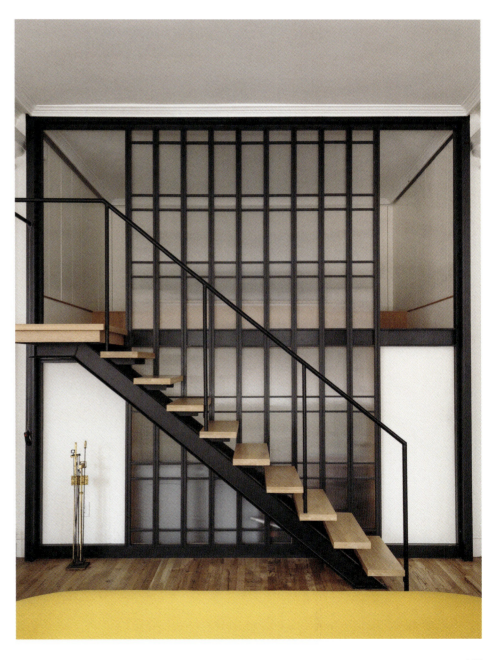

The yellow sofa from FAIR brings a jolt of color to the living room. A custom chandelier is made of hand-blown glass globes and is from Woka

A collection of personal items, including the couple's coveted record collection, fill the shelves in the living room

→

The platform bed
in oak was designed
by 2Michaels &
Jeffrey English and
was produced by
Aspen Interiors

A simple, neutral
aesthetic takes over
the bathroom

NEW THREADS

A soulful Tribeca apartment drenched in history underwent a hastened refresh by architect Crina Arghirescu Rogard, with phenomenal results.

When international architect and interior designer Crina Arghirescu Rogard was asked to polish a mutual friend's historic Tribeca apartment in just six weeks, she accepted the challenge without hesitation. "Limitations in architecture and life, to me, are moments for new discoveries," says Arghirescu Rogard. The mutual friend, artist Claudia Doring Baez, was preparing to host a party in honor of her participation in Volta New York and recruited Arghirescu Rogard to help modernize the apartment that she and her family had lived in for nearly ten years. "She wanted a completely new look. She wanted it to be functional and then beautiful at the same time," says Arghirescu Rogard.

The apartment resides on the top floor of the American Thread Building, a historic structure designed by William B. Tubby in the late 1800s. Mosaic flooring, a stained glass skylight, Renaissance Revival columns, moldings, and black walnut wall paneling are a few of the many architectural elements that have aged with grace throughout the apartment. Additionally, it is told that Baez's own living room was originally the American Thread Company's ballroom (known as "The Wool Club"), where titans of the fabric industry would convene to drink and dine. Arghirescu Rogard immediately sought to capture this unique history and intertwine it into the modernized design narrative, with playful, new furnishings and textural finishes.

Arghirescu Rogard began by studying the colors and tones within the large-scale Rose Wylie diptyque, 'Dot and Detail', that hung central in the dining room. Arghirescu Rogard playfully instilled this minimal palette of black, bright yellow, and ash blue into the rest of the design and throughout the customized furnishings, rugs and collaborative pieces. In the living room, the pre-existing shabby chic furnishings were replaced with an

'Manuel Gonzàlez, my great great grandfather, President of Mexico 1880-1884' by Claudia Doring Baez hangs above 'Lympho', a lounge chair by Taras Zheltyshev. The floor lamp is by Patrick E. Naggar

"They have this very strong common element in their family, which is art," says Arghirescu Rogard.

alligator-inspired custom sofa, a Franco Albini 'Fiorenza' lounge chair, and a neutral 'Lympho' chair by Taras Zheltyshev. Yellow, brightly hued resin cubes, produced by artist Liz Hopkins, define the malleable (and stackable) coffee table. A more neutral rug, lined in yellow, was chosen for its likeness to the original mosaic flooring inlaid in the apartment's foyer and the ceiling moldings.

Opposite the living room, the dining room hosts an array of custom, one-of-a-kind pieces, like the interconnected sky-blue chairs, hemmed together by loose fabric by artist Liz Collins. "It's a beautiful poetic piece," says Arghirescu Rogard. The chairs, all designed by Collins, are tucked under a custom resin table designed by Arghirescu Rogard in collaboration with artist Liz Hopkins. In the primary bedroom, Arghirescu Rogard customized a large, sculptural headboard finished in a dark green velvet, pairing the design with a raku ceramic and brushed steel coffee table from her own furniture collection.

The custom resin cubes are by artist Liz Hopkins. The 'Fiorenza' armchair is by Franco Albini and the painting (left) is by Claudia Doring Baez

The mix of original works of art, custom furnishings, and vintage pieces create an inspiring environment. "They have this very strong common element in their family, which is art," says Arghirescu Rogard, who creatively enhanced, curated, and customized each room to perfectly reflect her client and her family's delightfully colorful and artistic lives – just in time to party.

The mix of original works
of art, custom furnishings,
and vintage pieces create
an inspiring environment.

'Dot and Detail' by Rose Wylie is exhibited in the dining
room. A sculpture by Matias Di Carlo sits on a custom
resin table designed by Crina Arghirescu Rogard
in collaboration with artist Liz Hopkins

A pair of custom training poufs by Martine Rubenstein
and a Le Corbusier 'LC4' lounge chair sit under
an artwork by Claudia Doring Baez

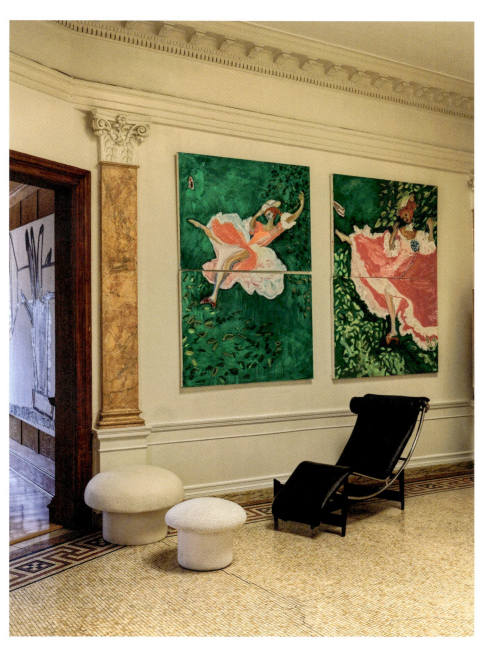

Artwork by Roy Oxlade is on display above the 'Manhattan' desk by Hélène de Saint Lager from Twenty First Gallery

'Claudia's Chairs' by artist Liz Collins add a splash of color and texture to the dining room

→

In the bathroom,
nearly every inch
of space is covered
in art and gently
shaded by a lush tree

In the primary bedroom, art from Lucero Gonzáles, Rose Wylie, and Lucero Gonzáles (left to right) adorns the wall. A custom headboard designed by Crina Arghirescu Rogard and a 'raku' table add playful textures to the room

POETRY IN COLOR

A vibrant collection of designs, new and old, were curated by architect Crina Arghirescu Rogard to transform a basic Tribeca loft into an inspiring work of art.

"It's a poetry of materials," says Crina Arghirescu Rogard, a Bucharest-born, Italian-educated architect, who launched her own design firm, Crina Arghirescu Rogard Architecture, in New York in 2013, shortly after working in Paris for several years. Historical furniture, contemporary artist collaborations, vividly hued custom installations, and repurposed materials are just a few of the ecstatic designs that Arghirescu Rogard playfully infused within her client's spacious Tribeca apartment.

The Tribeca project was one of a kind from the beginning. The client, Simon Elkaim, a real estate developer, and his wife, Kirsten Elkaim, wanted a completely new look, doused in vibrant, contrasting colors for Simon, who is partially colorblind. He has owned the apartment since 2009 and desired an authentic, bold palette that spoke to his condition and their colorful lives. "Before it had a different character... it didn't have the character it has now.

It has a whole other feeling," says Kirsten, a multidisciplinary artist and producer.

To begin, Arghirescu Rogard creatively reimagined the apartment's first impressions by installing custom poli-mirror steel doors at both ends of the hallway. Reclaimed wood once used on French railroads was chosen for the flooring, which continues throughout the rest of the apartment. The neutral, warm wood tone and white walls then set the stage for the vibrant installations and colorful pieces that await in every room.

In the kitchen, Arghirescu Rogard and Simon closely collaborated with Italian artist Henry Timi to design a kitchen island that is functional, yet a work of art. To that end, the artist designed a pair of semi-circular brushed stainless steel kitchen islands. "The

A vintage glass coffee table from the 1970s from UP&UP sits next to a Joe Colombo 'Model 4801' lounge chair for Kartell. The marble sculpture, 'Folded Shirts', is on display on the coffee table and is by Louis Sarowsky

133

"You can feel like it's a reflection of the creativity and art we both love," says Kirsten.

kitchen is the most important place in the unit, it's a living place," says Simon. Across from the kitchen lies the dining table made of burnt wood, also designed by Henry Timi. Above it, a wild, eclectic work of art by Barcelona-based artist Guillermo Santomà lights the room in an array of hues. "It's very colorful and unexpected, which is kind of a signature of both of us," says Kirsten.

In the living room, views of downtown Manhattan are framed within the floor-to-ceiling windows, providing an elegant backdrop to the mix of designer furnishings and original art that fill the room. At first glance, a custom Joris Poggioli 'Rose' sofa commands a playful space in the layout, accompanied by a floor lamp by Luigi Caccia Dominioni, a bright red customized bookshelf designed in collaboration with artist Liz Hopkins, and a stainless steel laser-cut sculpture by Daniela Palimariu. The joyful mix of installations, vintage furniture, and original works of art continue into the primary bedroom, where a pair of Joe Colombo vintage lounge chairs for Kartell (reupholstered in Holly Hunt's 'Hair-on-Hide' leather) sit across from a Hernan Ardila Delgado headboard. The primary bathroom is delicately sectioned off by an elegant glass wall, designed by Henry Timi, to reveal a Yves Klein-inspired blue resin tub (customized in close collaboration with Brooklyn-based designer Quincy Ellis from Facture Studio). Next to the customized bathtub, beautiful stonework frames the shower and sink, which was also imagined and customized by Henry Timi. The Yves Klein hue was a must from Simon, whose illustrious Tel Aviv home is completely doused in the historic color.

Perfectly curated by Arghirescu Rogard with (and for) her adventurous and delightful clients, the Tribeca apartment amuses and inspires. "You can feel like it's a reflection of the creativity and art we both love," adds Kirsten, "It's a very alive space, and Simon and I have a lot of life."

A Crina Arghirescu Architecture custom bookshelf, in collaboration with artist Liz Hopkins, is filled with personal items from the owners. The daybeds, also by Crina Arghirescu Architecture, move around the space. The painting, 'Roland Barthes', is by Claudia Doring Baez

135

"He's a brilliant architect
and artist at the same time,"
says Arghirescu Rogard,
of artist Guillermo Santomà,
who created the sculptural
chandelier.

In the living room, the painting 'Brassai study' ← ←
by Claudia Doring Baez (left) hangs next to
the 'Rose' sofa by Joris Poggioli and the 'Scrap Poly
Blue' chair by Max Lamb for Studio 94. The 'Giorgio
II' coffee table is by Francesco Balzano and
the 'Azucena Imbuto' floor lamp by Luigi
Caccia Dominioni

A Henry Timi custom burnt oak dining table is below ←
a custom chandelier by artist Guillermo Santomà,
titled 'Cerralbo'

A vintage Italian reupholstered armchair and floor ↓
lamp lie next to a photograph by Catinca Malaimare

Artwork by Claudia
Doring Baez hangs
above a custom bed
designed by Crina
Arghirescu
Architecture

A Henry Timi
custom brushed
stainless steel
kitchen counter
gently reflects its
surroundings,
including the Max
Lamb 'Scrap Poly
Blue' chair for
Studio 94 (left)

← ←

A Hernan Ardila headboard, 'Model 4801' Joe Colombo armchairs, and a pair of vintage 'Parola' sconces by Gae Aulenti & Piero Castiglioni for Fontana Arte adorn the primary bedroom

←

Henry Timi customized the primary bathroom stonework

→

The resin bathtub was customized by Facture Studio. The vase is by artist Nedda Atassi

The stone sink was
designed and
customized by
Henry Timi

THINKING OF ART

After a young art collector moved into her family's empty loft in Tribeca, she partnered with designer, James Ramsey, of RAAD Studio, to reimagine the layout entirely.

When a loft in Tribeca became available within one couple's real estate portfolio, their daughter saw the perfect opportunity to reinvent the space to house her growing art collection and their family's casual gatherings. "We are a big family," says the daughter. "We wanted a space where people are always welcome to come in, lounge, talk, and observe art." The daughter tapped James Ramsey, founder of the architecture firm RAAD Studio, to reimagine the space into a comforting showcase of art, design, and furniture. "As soon as I met him, I felt like our styles kind of aligned," remembers the daughter.

Ramsey, whose journey into architecture is a fascinating story for another day, founded his New York-based award-winning interior and architecture firm in 2004. As made evident by the firm's prolific and varied design projects, the architect excels at recognizing opportunity in any environment. "It was sort of a confusing clutter of spaces that needed to be combined and rethought," remembers

Ramsey, after his first site visit to the 4,000 square foot loft. Ramsey and his team cleared the mishmash of walls, leaving the social spaces in the front of the apartment and placing the media and bedrooms in the back (away from the noise and abundance of light). The kitchen, dining, and living room's new open floor design provided the daughter with an expansive, yet minimized interior where she could rotate artworks from her budding collection around the gallery-like walls. "I'm a very visual person," says the daughter, who holds a graduate degree in art. "For me, I just wanted to see the art from every angle in the room."

Next, the firm brought in a simple palette of materials, inspired by the loft's industrial ambiance, to create a minimalistic, yet warm environment within the new spacious floor plan. The chairs and sofas were kept low and neutral, so the artwork could be seen at any angle, without interruption. In the dining room, a playful mix of chairs

An artwork by Eddie Martinez is on display in the living room. The 'Extra Rolled Back' lounge chair is by Studio Paolo Ferrari

"We wanted a space where people are always welcome to come in, lounge, talk, and observe art," says the daughter.

color the long wooden table. "Everyone has a favorite chair," says the daughter. "We just had fun with it, it's not too serious."

In another effort to bring in more warmth into the industrial space, Ramsey and the firm creatively introduced nature into the layout by placing mini gardens within the customized shelving that lines the wall. "The incorporation of nature was a nice and cool way that we were able to tie that to the client's heritage," says Ramsey, who worked closely with John Mini Distinctive Landscaping to mimic the natural landscapes and terrains of the client's homeland. "It's like my small piece of home in New York," says the daughter.

The primary bedroom exudes an elegant and sophisticated aesthetic. And the primary bathroom was built using organic materials, wood and stone, so the room would feel timeless and spa-like. "I think one of the most timeless things you can do is use the materials that Mother Nature gave us," says Ramsey.

The brushed brass stools (right) are from 1stDibs, and the 'Extra Rolled Back' lounge chairs are by Studio Paolo Ferrari from Good Colony

Ramsey and his team at RAAD Studio redesigned a puzzling loft into a spacious, cozy home where the family (and its art) can easily hang.

The chairs and sofas were kept low and neutral, so the artwork could be seen at any angle, without interruption.

The 'Julep' sofa (left) is from Matter. The walnut coffee table is handcrafted and from 1stDibs. The white sectional is from Living Divani ← ←

Over the dining table (customized by Reko Brooklyn), the 'Phase. 03' chandelier from Anony lights the room. Chairs from DWR and Soft Chair color the space ←

A polished Ocean Grey stone from ABC Stone makes up the countertops and part of the kitchen island. The stool is from Artek ↓

←

The 'Puffer' chair (center) is from Moving Mountains. The sofa (left) is from Rove Concept, while the side table is part of Jasper Morrison's Cork Family for Vitra, and the Fort Standard coffee table is from Good Colony

→

In the bedroom, the 'Manti BS' floor lamp from BWR lights the bed from RH. The 'Poodle' side table is from 1stDibs

The 'Light Rods'
chandelier from
West Elm is hung
over the soaking tub
from Ruvati.
The stone in the
bathroom is Ceppo
De Gri and was
sourced from
ABC Stone

04

BROWNSTONE DREAMS

Through the thoughtful care and vision from owner Hallie Morrison and architect Jane Kim, a 19th-century brownstone was thoughtfully restored to enjoy yet another historic century in the heart of Brooklyn's Fort Greene.

Hallie Morrison and Seth Frader-Thompson's search for a three-bedroom apartment serendipitously landed the couple in a 19th-century brownstone in the charming neighborhood of Fort Greene, Brooklyn. This perfect find on a perfect street was received in not-so-perfect condition. The five-story townhouse was cut up into four separate apartments, dressed sporadically in stained mustard shag carpet, vinyl floors, and turquoise walls. "It was actually in pretty rough shape, which was a little sad, but also nice... You have more of a blank slate to start where you want," says Morrison, a landscape architect and designer. The couple soon realized they needed help to properly restore the historic structure's partially erased facade and decaying interior. Morrison discovered Jane Kim, of Jane Kim Architect, through a friend. Kim was quick to pick up the scope of work and helped the couple restore, preserve, and modernize their crumbling brownstone, inside and out.

Built in 1879, the brownstone is set at the end of four adjoining houses, with large windows welcoming light from three different walls – a rare treat for any New York apartment. The home's facade, when purchased, was partially embellished with detailed architectural moldings from the late 20th century, yet they appeared as if they were partially erased. Kim and their contractor worked to bring the fading detailing back to its original state, which they were able to do by observing the neighboring brownstones. Behind the facade, they discovered and enhanced the home's original base moldings, wooden walnut staircase, wooden banisters, entry archway, marble fireplace, and wooden windows.

A marble mantel adorns the fireplace on the first floor ←

When it came to filling the home, Morrison and Frader-Thompson thoughtfully curated an aesthetic and layout that uniquely reflected their own habits, practical

Once construction began, the team discovered the walls were still coated in horse hair plaster – a material commonly used in the early 1900s and that does indeed include horse hair in the mix.

necessities, and personalized comforts. "One thing that was instilled in me is how you use a house," says Morrison, who carries her own family's design torch passed on to her from her father (who was an industrial designer for Knoll), who received it from his father (who worked for Robert Moses, one of New York's most influential urban planners in the early 20th century).

The couple wanted the kitchen, dining, and living room to easily welcome and host their family and friends. Kim helped the couple realize this by removing the walls on the parlor floor and enlarging the back facade, which amplified the light throughout the entire floor and granted easy access to the back garden and deck. The design allowed for an organic and fluid transition between cooking, dining, and lounging. Morrison then sprinkled in furniture, new, old, and found, within the open layout, which creatively sectioned off each designated space. Kim continued to design layouts on each floor that allowed the light to travel organically and uninterrupted, while giving the option to privatize and section off rooms as needed. "We wanted our home to be more like an assemblage and something that is going to continue over time," says Morrison. The brownstone's perfectly imperfect history is now folded into a charming revival story that was written and made to last.

A pair of glass globes from Allied Maker light the island in the kitchen ←

"One thing that was instilled in me is how you use a house," says Morrison, a third-generation designer.

A sophisticated mix of textures and hues fill the living room next to the entry ← ←

A linear light by Apparatus is hung over a wooden dining table ←

The staircase and banisters were original to the home and restored by Jane Kim Architect ↓

◄ ◄

The lush, green
backyard is filled
with mostly native
plants. "It's kind
of my experimental
play space," says
Morrison

◄

The verdant-cast
kitchen exudes
a natural, earthy
aesthetic

➔

The window panels
and shutters
were restored
to their original
glory throughout
the house

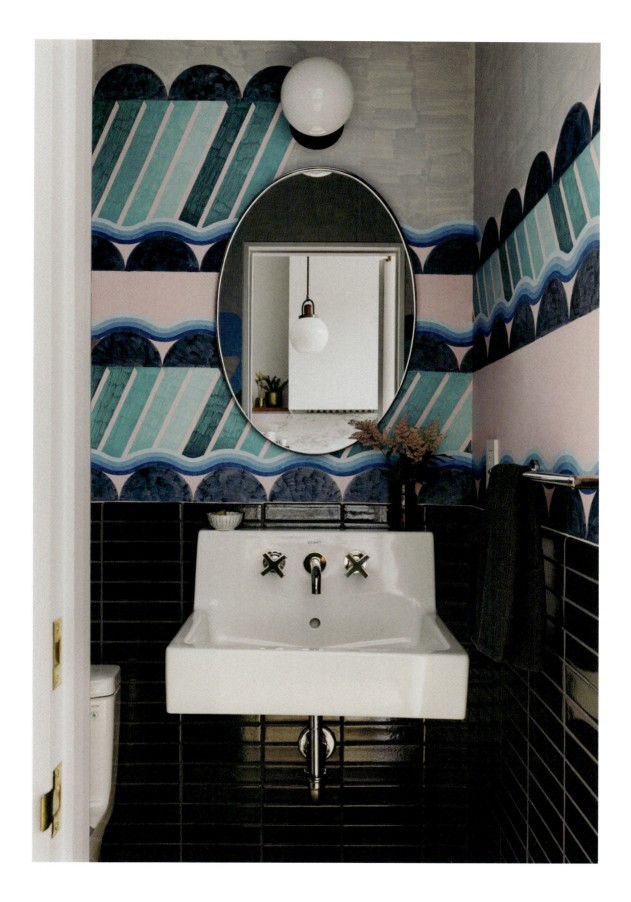

A hand-painted
mural by Mark
Joshua Epstein
adds color to
the downstairs
powder room

A NATURAL REFLECTION

A first-time home buyer recruits interior designer, Stefania Skrabak, to personalize her new apartment in Boerum Hill.

"When do you know?" An intuitive question that can weave potential home buyers in and out a myriad of empty properties until the answer reveals itself in plain sight. For Leah Sauter, a first-time home buyer and Pacific Northwest native, the "knowing" was the hardest part, until it wasn't. "I remember walking in, and in the first 20 seconds thinking, 'I have to have this!,'" recalls Sauter. The "must-have" transitional townhouse boasted 15.5-foot ceiling heights, breathtaking floor-to-ceiling windows, and a private rooftop overlooking Brooklyn and beyond. The property is also nestled within Saint Marks Place, a newly developed residential building designed by INC Architecture & Design, built to honor the architectural language of Boerum Hill's iconic brownstone-lined streets.

Soon after Sauter acquired her dream home, in her dream neighborhood, she began looking for someone to help personalize her beautiful, yet bare, three-bedroom home. The lawyer organically clicked with the work of Stefania

Skrabak, an artist, self-taught interior designer, and Principal Designer of Art Home Garden, LLC / AHG Interiors. Skrabak's elevated, earthy aesthetics and Sauter's desire for a cozy interior made for a perfect match. "This is one of the first designs that I felt truly connected to as a designer and as an artist," remembers Skrabak.

When entering the apartment, the living room's 15-foot windows overlooking Saint Marks Place frame a beautiful white oak tree on the street. "I didn't really need to look for more inspiration other than this tree," says Skrabak. Using nature as the inspiration was innately welcomed by Sauter, who lives miles away from her childhood home in Washington state, where the forested terrain and mountainous landscapes were an everyday backdrop. "The outdoors, greenery, and nature – all of this plays a central part of everybody's day-to-day lived experience, and I like that Stefania was able to bring that into my home," says Sauter.

In the living room, a painting by Michael McGrath is on display over a console table. The carpet is by Nina Freudenberger from Lulu and Georgia

"This is one of the first designs that I felt truly connected to as a designer and as an artist," remembers Stefania Skrabak.

Beginning in the living room, an immaculate (in artistry and scale) bespoke Grizedale Green mural was fastened to one side of the wall. The open floor plan, which is subtly defined by a playful mix of furnishing arrangements, became the perfect hosting space for Sauter, who cooks and entertains often. "It's a very seamless setup for people to spend time here," says Sauter.

In the kitchen, Skrabak worked alongside the pre-existing materials and design, like the wood veneer cabinets and white oak flooring (which were curated and installed by the developers) and continued the picturesque landscape mural into the kitchen. The wallpaper, which is 15 feet tall and 30 feet wide, was carefully laid so the trees and shrubbery were perfectly framed in all the right places. "The trees give the kitchen so much more life. A kitchen should be apple pie and chocolate chip cookies. In a weird way, it gives it that feeling," says Skrabak.

The primary bedroom, office, and guest room host a comforting mix of vintage finds alongside store-bought furnishings, with more vegetal wallpaper in the background. "I really like a mix of high and low," says Skrabak, who explores the pages of 1stDibs, Etsy, and contemporary furnishing makers as she considers and edits each space.

Skrabak personalized every inch of the home to reflect her client's tastes. "I feel like it's very uniquely me and tied to my interests and how I want to live more so than I think I was able to articulate to Stefania," says Sauter. "It looks like it belongs here and was always here."

In the dining room, Marcel Breuer-style vintage rattan dining chairs from 1stDibs are nestled under a dining table and flanked by a pair of green accent chairs (both from Rejuvenation). The chandelier is from Art Home Garden Shop

"The outdoors, greenery, and nature – all of this plays a central part of everybody's day-to-day lived experience, and I like that Stefania was able to bring that into my home," says Sauter.

In the living room, an artwork by Michael McGrath (right), a vintage tapestry from 1stDibs, and forested wall covering from Graham & Brown adorn the walls ← ←

Unique furnishings, art, and one-of-a-kind designs creatively partition each room in the open floor plan ←

The sofa is from RH and the sconces were discovered on Etsy ↓

← ←

The outdoor furniture on the rooftop overlooking the skyline is from RH

←

Skrabak creatively incorporated the existing wide oak floors and Luca di Luna quartzite countertops and backsplash into her new design. The handmade wood veneer pendants were found on Etsy and the counter stools were sourced from CB2

→

A vintage 'Togo' chair takes over the corner in the primary bedroom

The soothing and elegant bathroom was designed by the building's developers, INC Architecture & Design

→

The guest bedroom
hosts a bed from
Lulu and Georgia,
with a Le Corbusier
checkered throw
blanket, and
wallpaper from
Farrow & Ball.
The bedside tables
and chandelier
are vintage

A checkered rug adds a splash of color and pattern to the office. The wooden desk was customized and made in Poland

PARIS À BROOKLYN

After finally finding the perfect blank box on a beautiful street in Brooklyn, the owners tapped interior designer Jae Joo to help them beautify the home, inside and out.

When first-time home buyers Lindsay Nelson and Kayvan Salmanpour began the search for their (eventual) family home, they kept the filter simple. "We were really looking for a shell on a beautiful block," says Nelson, a marketing and technology executive, who discovered their dream home on a tree-lined street in the heart of Fort Greene, Brooklyn. Built in the early 20th century, their new townhouse was just a block from Fort Greene Park, rose four stories high, and included a private backyard – it was perfect. Inside, however, was a different story. "It was the ugliest house you could ever imagine inside," laughs Nelson.

As soon as the couple had the keys, they began their search for a designer. "We were looking for someone who really shared our aesthetic and had an appreciation for mixing new and old and not having a very rigid style," remembers Nelson. Nelson and Salmanpour, a media executive, were soon introduced to Jae Joo, founder of the New York-based interior designer studio Jae Joo Designs. When they met with Joo, the couple expressed their desire for a metamorphic design, one that could easily transform as their family and lifestyles would eventually evolve. "We wanted a space that was really flexible for the family that we imagined we were going to grow into but that didn't make design compromises in the spirit of practicality," says Nelson. Joo and the couple agreed that a gut renovation (keeping just the staircase and a fireplace or two) was the best place to start. "Usually, I am all about keeping historic details... this wasn't that," says Joo.

With a clean slate, the magic began. On the first floor, an atypical layout was turned into a more convenient and practical flow for the family. The dining room was moved to the front towards the entrance, the kitchen shuffled to the center of the home, and the living room went to the back. "The kitchen became absolutely the center of the home, and we entertain all of the time, so it was just this really

In the living room, the fireplace was plastered by Kamp Studios. The artwork is by Matías Sánchez Martín, and lit by a sconce from Circa Lighting. The chair and coffee table are from BDDW

187

> "We wanted a space that was really flexible for the family that we imagined we were going to grow into but that didn't make design compromises in the spirit of practicality," says Nelson.

unusual but super smart decision that completely defined the character of the home," says Nelson. "It worked perfectly in practice."

In the living room, Joo proposed a cylindrical fireplace topped with a fluted plastered surface. "Everything kind of stemmed from that fireplace," recalls Joo, who then brought the clients' desired "Paris meets Brooklyn" theme into each architecturally lacking floor. Plaster walls, rounded arches, steel French doors, white oak floors (in beautiful herringbone), crown moldings, and aged bronze accents were installed, becoming the foundation for the rest of the design. "We wanted the house to look great with nothing in it," says Joo.

The primary bedroom only allowed space for the couple's bed, an unexpected architectural challenge that the couple then embraced by moving the closet storage to the bathroom and keeping the bedroom simple, minimal, and all about the views and sleeping. The guest bathroom, which was designed to also inspire the imagination of future children (the couple now has two), was dressed in a forested wallpaper, storm-hued cement tiles, and a farmhouse sink. Joo continued this playful design narrative, seeped in European charm, throughout each room.

Every piece of furniture nestled in this charming corner is from BDDW ←

"For us, it was such an amazing project," says Nelson, whose trust in Joo's creative vision produced a charming first home that mirrors the creative couple's sophisticated lens on modern life.

"We wanted the house to
look great with nothing in it,"
says Joo.

In the kitchen, a geometric chandelier from Flos lights the ← ←
marble island. The stools were sourced from BDDW

An abstract artwork by Tyler Hays is on display in the ←
dining room. The chairs, table, and rug are from BDDW

The banister and stairwell were lightly refreshed ↓
and restored

← ←

In the office, the chairs and 'Bear' rug (from BDDW) add to the playful, linear aesthetic that surrounds

←

Herringbone wood floors add a charming tone to the home's simplified palette

→

The primary bedroom comes with a private balcony overlooking the couple's backyard and neighborhood. The sculptures are by Jenny Min

The framed puzzle,
hung over
the primary bed,
was discovered
at BDDW

→

In the guest
bathroom, aging
bronze appliances
mingle with a classic
black and white
checkered floor

A whimsical wallcovering adds a bit of story and depth to the kids' bathroom

A FRESH START

Interior designer Jae Joo creatively updated her clients' industrial loft to better suit and gently welcome the couple's tiny newcomer.

In a 20th-century, former factory building on Wythe Street, a prominent Williamsburg street just a block away from the East River, lies the home of Brooke Hammel and Jose Alvarez. Alvarez, a co-owner of the fragrance company Abbott, purchased the open floor loft nearly a decade ago. At the time he and Hammel, a financier, tapped interior designer Jae Joo to help them redesign and gently polish their new 1,800 square foot apartment. "It was obvious the possibilities of what you could do with the height and original architecture," says Joo, who stuck with the loft's raw, industrial ambiance and designed a savvy, highly personalized home for her new clients to enjoy and share with their guests. Fast forward a few years and Joo, founder of Jae Joo Designs, is back on the job site with a new design agenda: make it a family home.

The couple wanted a softer atmosphere with more privacy, but a design that spoke to their (new) family and the loft's existing aesthetic. Joo left the large steel windows, unfinished brick and cement walls, paint-splattered floors (from artists past), and exposed columns all untouched. "There's all these unique features to the loft, so that all you really needed to do was give it a nice polish," says Joo. Joo worked on designing the second bedroom on the top floor to act as the nursery, enclosing the open stairwell, adding a bathroom, and an expansion for the primary bathroom – changes that would help make the daily flow of life more practical, safer, and enjoyable.

In the primary bathroom, custom shelving and a sculptural bathtub were added to the space, in the same aesthetic as the rest of the home. "We basically changed the master bathroom to fit the overall feel of the loft better," says Joo. The nursery equally reflects the loft's raw beauty. Here, Joo added plenty of storage and dressed the floors, walls, and crib in ultra-soft textures and fabrics to amplify the warmth and coziness.

A vintage stool holds a floral arrangement in the loft's entry ←

"There's all these unique features to the loft, so that all you really needed to do was give it a nice polish," says Jae Joo.

The living room and dining room are loosely sectioned off by a mix of traditional and transitional furnishings, like the extra-large sectional, large custom rug, linear dining table and chairs, and winged lounger. Joo found a home for the couple's colorful collection of tchotchkes picked up from their travels, books, framed artworks, and more on the large custom bookshelf on the living room wall. She also placed Alvarez's surfboards poetically in the mix. "We agreed that this loft should feel authentic to who they are and it should be filled with their personal items they love to live with," remembers Joo.

A custom coffee table, Flag Halyard lounge chair, a rug from Beauvais Carpets, and wooden shelving fill the living room ←

Within a year, the couple and Joo thoughtfully transformed a light-filled loft, attuned to the couple's colorful and cultured lifestyles, into a soothing family home perfectly equipped for their next chapter.

The couple wanted a softer atmosphere with more privacy, but a design that spoke to their (new) family and the loft's existing aesthetic.

A vintage Japanese denim blanket covers the sofa from Home Nature. Ceramics by Jenny Min adorn the dining table from RH. The chairs were discovered at BDDW ← ←

A photograph from Morrison Hotel Gallery is framed and displayed on the kitchen counter. The pendant is from Sonneman ←

Ceramics by Jenny Min are displayed on the RH dining table ↓

← ←

Additional storage
and an extra
bedroom were
included in the new
layout to make
room for the
couple's first child

←

The crib, from West
Elm, lies under
a tapestry, with
custom rugs
adorning the floor

→

The tub is from
Oceanstone and
all fittings are
by Zucchetti

In the primary
bedroom, the drapes
and linens are by
Romo Fabrics, the
sconce is from Arne
Jacobsen, the bed is
from RH, and the
candle is from
Abbott Fragrance

05

CHARM AND SOUL

When first-time homeowners Anaïs Katz and Simon Royaux toured a pre-war apartment drenched in natural light and dotted in period architecture, they quickly tapped Kevin Greenberg of Space Exploration to help modernize and preserve its authentic beauty.

After five months and viewing nearly a hundred apartments, Anaïs Katz and Simon Royaux finally found "the one" – a pre-war, three-bedroom apartment in an immaculate Haussmannian building on the Upper West Side. Every step, beginning at the lobby's Hollywood-esque elevator and into the apartment's delicately preserved architectural layout, was perfect for the couple who desperately wanted a space with a vivid history, European semblance, and natural charm. "There's a lot of love and thought and design that was clearly put into the bones of this apartment, and the building," says Katz, who remembers wanting the apartment before she and Royaux finished the entire tour. The high ceilings, ornate crown moldings, and enormous windows were a few of the many persuasions that eventually landed the couple in their new home.

Even though the apartment was sold at first sight, the century-old architectural features and appliances needed some conditioning, which led the couple to Kevin Greenberg, founding principal of Space Exploration, a design studio based in New York. To no one's surprise, the apartment's authentic beauty also lured in Greenberg at first sight. "The minute I walked in, I said to myself, 'we need to do this project.' I was really excited about it right away," recalls Greenberg. "In our projects, the most important characteristic is soul. That's what we are always seeking to achieve," he says. "And their apartment already had it."

Beginning at the entry, Greenberg's team installed a black and white checkered tile flooring to provide a more stylized partitioning before entering the rest of the home. The apartment's existing wooden floors were patterned and beautiful, but decaying, so the team installed thin, patterned, herringbone planks in their place. For the walls, a delicate white hue was chosen for the entire apartment, creating a calming backdrop for the couple's eclectic sensibilities.

In the living room, an artwork (created by the owners themselves) hangs framed above a Charlotte Perriand chair, upholstered in cowhide

The high ceilings, ornate crown moldings, and enormous windows were a few of the many persuasions that eventually landed the couple in their new home.

"There's a level of detail that you don't anticipate when you embark on this type of project," says Katz, "I loved it." Each room's buoyant mix of antique and refurbished furnishings was sourced by either Space Exploration or Katz and Royaux's vintage Italian furnishings expert, and every piece was carefully considered among the others to provide the couple with the perfect homecoming that authentically reflected their refined taste in art and culture. "We wanted the furniture to feel modern, but have a link to history, as our apartment does," says Katz.

The only structural change was the removal of a wall between the kitchen and third bedroom, which then allowed for a more spacious flow so the couple could more easily cook, host, and dine with friends and family. Top-notch appliances were also installed throughout the home to make the historic apartment fit for contemporary living. The apartment's alluring design and charming soul is now equipped for the 21st century and tastefully personalized to reflect Katz and Royaux's sophisticated nature.

A ceramic sconce in black clay, from In Common With, lights the kitchen's marble countertops ←

"In our projects, the most important characteristic is soul. That's what we are always seeking to achieve," says Greenberg. "And their apartment already had it."

In the living room, a custom bookshelf (designed by Space Exploration) holds the owner's colorful keepsakes. A Mario Bellini chair for B&B Italia adds a splash of color to the mix ← ←

The painting, by French artist Claude Viallat, hangs above the fireplace. The Paavo Tynell wicker floor lamp and Artek stool upholstered in vintage Alexander Girard fabric bring in a sense of warmth. The Pierre Jeanneret 'Kangaroo' chair is paired with a custom cushion ←

The entryway is lit by a double-angle brass pendant by Michael Anastassiades ↓

← ←

In the kitchen, vintage Bruno Rey chairs with custom cushions are tucked under a vintage dining table from 1stDibs

←

In the office, the desk chair (from BDDW) sits under a wooden desk. The artwork is by Bram van Velde and the table lamp is by Gino Sarfatti

→

Vintage stools from Brooklyn's Holler & Squall act as nightstands in the primary bedroom

A Ligne Roset 'Togo' chair offers additional seating in the office. The floor lamp is by Akari and the artwork is by Bram van Velde

→

The powder room
is the most colorful
room in the house,
doused in tadelakt in
a calming pale green
with square tiles
below

The chair, which belonged to the couple before they moved in, was reupholstered in a striped fabric from Zak and Fox. The artwork is by Etel Adnan

IN GOOD HANDS

A 20th-century row house in Queens underwent a three-year, hands-on renovation resulting in a complete transformation by design duo Erica Sellers and Jeremy Silberberg of Studio S II.

When Erica Sellers, a multidisciplinary artist and product designer, purchased a three-story row house in Ridgewood, Queens, she immediately called Jeremy Silberberg, her good friend and interior designer, to come check it out. As the two unfolded their own thoughts, ideas, and dreams into the space, it slowly became clear that this visit and those ideas were brewing towards something much bigger. "There was just a certain moment when it became apparent that we were completely aligned on the vision for the property," remembers Silberberg. Their naturally aligned aesthetics and passions for customized, nuanced design eventually formalized into a partnership, which they coined Studio S II. "It all happened simultaneously, our partnership, our connection, making work, starting to get clientele," recalls Sellers.

Seller's traditionally built 1912 New York house was their first Studio S II project, and became somewhat of a practice field where the artists would flesh out their ideas and newfound design firm. The row house, however, was "a box, like a rectangular prism," jokes Silberberg, who then sought to find any architectural integrity hidden underneath the layers of renovations past. To start, Silberberg uncovered 12-foot ceilings hidden above the home's hovering 7.5-foot ceiling panels, and preserved the existing skylights that let in uninterrupted light. In order to welcome in even more light, he and Sellers created a vantage point from the front door to the back, by opening up all the walls on the parlor floor. Additionally, they cut a hole into the second level above the entry's staircase, carving out a grander, sun-filled welcome.

When it came to the aesthetics and overall tone, Sellers and Silberberg began by creating a labyrinth of historical and personal images to reference. "It started with a lot of collaging," remembers Silberberg, who joined Sellers in pinning reference images

Studio S II produced the 'Scalp' sconce and 'Noli Me Tangere' church pew. The checkered side table is by Elana Shvalbe

"It all happened simultaneously, our partnership, our connection, making work, starting to get clientele," says Sellers.

from movies, of people, and paintings within each room, where they dissected and invented their way into an original design. The marble in the kitchen was chosen for its Cy Twombly-esque stone strokes, which was paired with custom barstools made with blackened steel spikes and oxblood leather cushions. They also revived and repurposed a Gothic Revival cabinet into a sink in the parlor bathroom and designed the entire breakfast area as an homage to a boiler room they both adored that appears in the *Spirited Away* movie. The antiques around the home are almost exclusively Renaissance or Gothic Revival pieces, which were paired with contemporary works of art and collectible designs to create a well-tempered juxtaposition.

Sellers and Silberberg eventually (and organically) came to the idea that the home should act as a gallery for their studio, where they could showcase their work among their peers, collaborators, and other artists. "All of these design decisions and moves happened very gradually," says Silberberg. And the transition of the home into a partial showroom "just evolved," recalls Sellers. "It just turned into the entire ethos of our company and our creative voices. It was very natural. The evolution was just so natural that it became obvious at a certain point that this is our stage," says Silberberg.

The 'Belial' barstools, ←
made with oxblood
leather and
blackened steel, are
by Studio S II

From a plain box to an original work of art, Sellers and Silberberg designed a home like no other – a perfect reflection of Studio S II.

"The home just turned into the entire ethos of our company and our creative voices. It was very natural. The evolution was just so natural that it became obvious at a certain point that this is our stage," says Silberberg.

On the second floor, artworks and designs by Lauren Goodman, Susannah Weaver, Caroline Chao, Benjamin Kapoor, Luke Malaney, and Studio S II surround a custom rug by Katie Stout ←

'Six Spheres' by Dom Smith are hung next to a chair by Sebastian Arroyo Hoebens ↓

←←

On the second floor,
a chair by Ryan
Decker sits under
a work of art by
Benjamin Kapoor

←

Above the bed, a
work by Studio S II
is hung between
illuminated metal
cabinets by Jeff
Goodman

→

On the wall, a work
by Jeremy Martin
titled 'LAND/
ESCAPE' is hung
above a sculpture by
Caroline Zimbalist,
a chair by Studio S
II, and a five-legged
console table by
J. Mcdonald

The 'Bryophyte'
pedestal table
doubles as a
nightstand in the
primary bedroom

→

A pair of 'Eclipse'
sconces by Roll
& Hill light the
custom vanity in the
primary bathroom

↑

Above the primary
bed, an artwork
by Rebecca Manson
takes center stage

AN UPPER EAST SIDE GEM

A newly built apartment on the Upper East Side has become the perfect family pied-à-terre thanks to interior designer Charlotte Sylvain.

"It was totally a blank canvas," says the French-born, New York-based designer Charlotte Sylvain, of her client's new three-bedroom residence on the Upper East Side. Her clients, a couple from Pennsylvania with three adult children, purchased the apartment on 88th Street to function as their family's pied-à-terre and the occasional crash pad when the husband came into town for work. Sylvain was introduced to the out-of-town clients through a mutual real estate agent. The wife recalls her thoughts when she first laid eyes on Sylvain's portfolio: "I said, wow this makes sense, clean lines, modern. It had all the sensibilities."

Located in Carnegie Hill, the building was designed and developed by DDG, and inspired by New York's historic 20th-century architecture and designs. The developers collaborated with experienced craftsmen and designers including the Denmark-based masonry firm Petersen Tegl, which crafted the handmade bricks seen on the building's exterior, and Molteni & C Dada, an Italian luxury design studio, which designed the stately kitchens. Sylvain honed in on the developers reinvented, historic architecture, which is delicately paired with modern-day craftsmanship, and designed a space where her clients could relax easily, host friends and family often, and savor the city's epic skyline views from any vantage point in the home.

Beginning in the living room, "the idea was to do something minimalist," says Sylvain. An extra-large sofa, designed by Stahl + Band sheathed in Sherpa fabric, takes over the corner, with a bar cart, designed by Alvar Aalto, to add a bit of history and geometry to the space. Sylvain also made sure the overall design felt warm and did so by introducing natural fiber into the material palette and brightening the rooms with paper shade lighting.

The coffee table and sofa were sourced from Stahl + Band. The artwork is by Allen Hansen

Between the living room and kitchen, a two-tone custom dining table was designed by Fort Standard, a local design

"At night, when you put the big lanterns on and the windows are open and blinds are up, it's amazing," says the owner.

studio and manufacturer based in Brooklyn. Sylvain also customized a small bar behind the dining table, for when dinner guests keep arriving and the dinner table is full. The bar is furnished with four barstools produced by the Los Angeles-based design studio Estudio Persona. "I love the shape of the barstools. I thought they were so cool and add a bit of organic feel because they are rounded to break up everything being so linear," says Sylvain.

The primary bedrooms and two additional guest bedrooms capture, yet again, Sylvain's natural talent for breathing color, light, and life into an empty, white box. Each room keeps the minimal, clean-lined tone, but gently breaks away from the black and white aesthetic set within the social spaces. White draperies, rattan, honey-toned wood, varying black and white artworks, and earth-toned textures mix and mingle in each room, creating individualized, sophisticated sleeping quarters.

A pair of lounge chairs from Menu and a rug from Armadillo add a cozy texture to the living room. The pendants are from &Tradition, barstools are from Estudio Persona, and the custom bar table is by Current Flow Woodwork

"Sylvain was so easy because she knew what she was doing," says the client, who delighted in the design process with Sylvain, and enjoys the final outcome with friends and family as much as possible. "At night, when you put the big lanterns on and the windows are open and blinds are up, it's amazing," she adds.

Located in Carnegie Hill, the building was designed and developed by DDG, and inspired by New York's historic 20th-century architecture and designs.

Romantic views of Manhattan are seen through the ← ←
living room windows. The sofa and coffee tables are from
Stahl + Band, while the bar cart (left) is by Alvar Aalto

The two-tone dining table was made by Fort Standard ←
and the dining chairs are from Nikari. The kitchen was
existing and designed by Molteni & C Dada, an Italian
luxury design studio, for the building's developers, DDG

Views of New York City's skyline are framed throughout ↓
the apartment

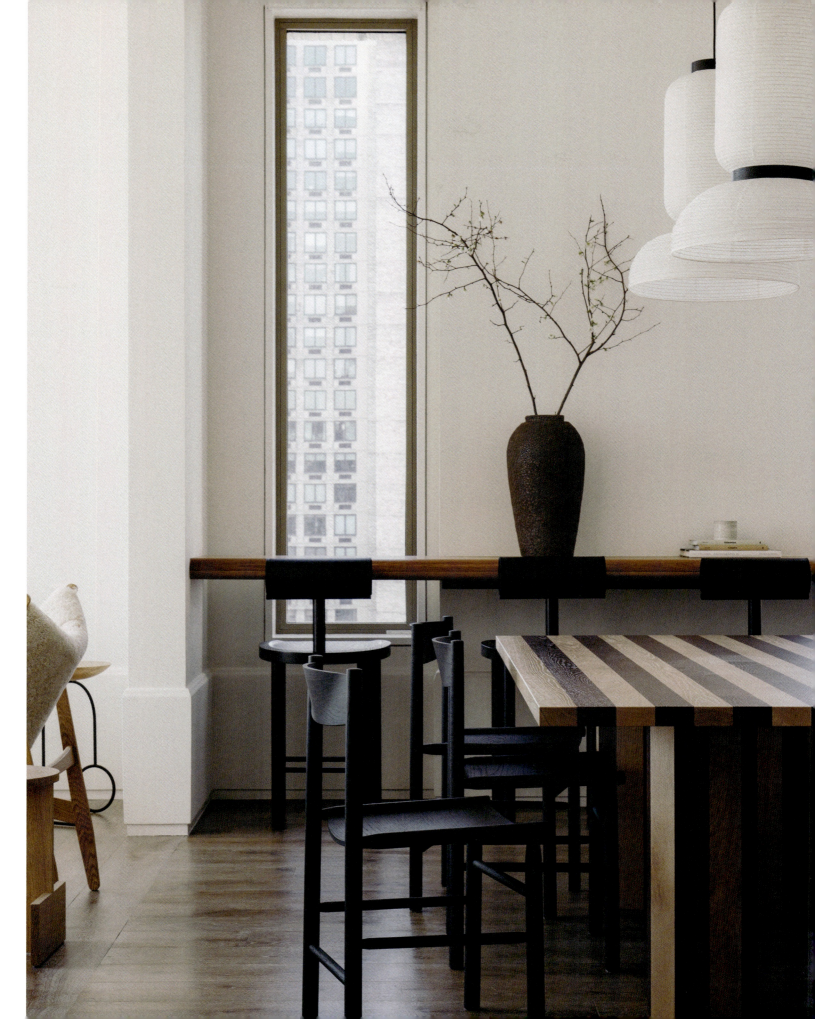

← ←

The dining room sits
between the kitchen
and living room and
hosts a bold, playful
mix of custom
seating for the
owner's family
and guests

←

Barstools are from
Estudio Persona,
paper pendants are
from &Tradition,
dining chairs are
by Nikari, and the
table was customized
by Current Flow
Woodwork

→

The bathroom design
was original to the
apartment and hosts
a soothing, earthy
aesthetic

↑

Artwork by Allen
Hansen hangs over
a bed from
Industry West.
The nightstands are
from Faithful Roots
and the lamps are
from HK Living

CREDITS

CHASING THE LIGHT
PP. 8 & 10-21
Architect: GRT Architects
grtarchitects.com
@grtarchitects
Stylist: Ridge House
Photography: Nicole Franzen
nicolefranzen.com
@nicole_franzen

DIVINE DESIGN
PP. 22-35
Owner: Marcee Smith
Architecture and Interior Design:
Robert Marinelli
@robertmarinellidesign
robertmarinelli.com
Photography: Joseph Kramm
josephkramm.com
@joeinstakramm

GOING BANANAS
PP. 36-45
Owner: Manuela Giannini
Interior Designer: Alex P White
alexpwhite.com
@alexpwhite
Stylist: Jennifer Brown
aleisuresport.com
@aleisuresport
Strauss Bourque-Lafrance
straussbourquelafrance.com
@straussbourquelafrance
Photography: Chris Mottalini
mottalini.com
@chrismottalini

EAST TO WEST
PP. 48-61
Interior Designer: Francis Toumbakaris,
Francis Interiors
francisinteriors.com
@francisinteriors
Architecture Firm: Soluri Architecture
@soluri_architecture

soluri-architecture.com
Landscape architect:
Viewpoints Design
Stylist: Robert Rufino
@therobertrufino
Photography: Joseph Kramm
josephkramm.com
@joeinstakramm

IN THE WAKE
OF LEGACY
PP. 46 & 62-73
Inhabitant: The Future Perfect,
New York
thefutureperfect.com
@thefutureperfect
@davidalhadeff
Architect: David Chipperfield
Photography: Joseph Kramm
josephkramm.com
@joeinstakramm

NEW BEGINNINGS
PP. 74-83
Interior Designer: Julia Blanchard
of Blanchard Design
blancharddesignllc.com
@booblanchard
Architect: Selldorf Architects
Photography: Nick Glimenakis
nickglimenakis.com
@nickglimenaki

CHELSEA DREAMING
PP. 84-95
Owners: Paige and Ben Zachs
Interior Designer: Tali Roth,
Studio Tali Roth
studiotaliroth.com
@studiotaliroth
Stylist: Mieke ten Hae
Photography: Nick Glimenakis
nickglimenakis.com
@nickglimenakis

A CHELSEA STORY
PP. 96-107
Owners: Kristina O'Neal and Adam
Gordon
Photography: Joseph Kramm
josephkramm.com
@joeinstakramm

TWO OF A KIND
PP. 110-121
Interior Designers: Jayne Michaels
and Joan Michaels, 2 Michaels Design
2michaelsdesign.com
@2michaelsdesign
Architectural Designer:
Jeffrey English
Construction: Aspen Interior
aspeninteriorllc.com
Photography: Matthew Williams
matthewwilliamsphotographer.com
@matthewwilliamsphotographer

NEW THREADS
PP. 108 & 122-131
Owner: Claudia Doring Baez
Interior Designer: Crina Arghirescu
Rogard of Crina Arghirescu
Rogard Architecture
crina-architecture.com
crina_architecture
Photography: Chris Mottalini
mottalini.com
@chrismottalini

POETRY IN COLOR
PP. 132-145
Owners: Simon & Kirsten Elkaim
Architecture and Interior Design:
Crina Arghirescu Rogard of Crina
Arghirescu Rogard Architecture
crina-architecture.com
@crina_architecture
Team: Axelle Dechelette, Tim Batellino,
Franchesca Rousseas, Léa Pernet
Art Liaison: Franchesca Popescu,

FPI Art Initiative
Photography: Chris Mottalini
mottalini.com
@chrismottalini

THINKING OF ART
PP. 6 & 146-157
Architect: James Ramsey,
RAAD Studio
Lead Architect: Alessandra Travaini
raadstudio.com
@raad_studio
Landscape Design: John Mini,
Distinctive Landscaping
Photography: Nick Glimenakis
nickglimenakis.com
@nickglimenakis

BROWNSTONE DREAMS
PP. 160-171
Owners: Hallie Morrison
and Seth Frader-Thompson
Architect: Jane Kim,
Jane Kim Architect
janekimarchitect.com
@jane_kim_architect
Photography: Nick Glimenakis
nickglimenakis.com
@nickglimenakis

A NATURAL REFLECTION
PP. 172-185
Owner: Leah Sauter
Interior Designer: Stefania Skrabak of
Art Home Garden LLC, AHG Interiors
@arthomegarden
arthomegarden.com
Architect: INC Architecture
& Design
Inc.nyc
Building Owner: Shlomi Avdoo
avdoo.com
Stylist: Victoria Maiolo

@victoria_maiolo
victoriamaiolo.com
Landscaper: John Cody
of Metrocrest Landscaping
Metrocrestlandscape.com
Build: Ben Nunn and Margarito
Flores of Dum Designs
Dumdesigns.com
@dumdesignsllc
Photography: Nick Glimenakis
nickglimenakis.com
@nickglimenakis

PARIS À BROOKLYN
PP. 186-199
Owners: Lindsay Nelson
and Kayvan Salmanpour
Interior Designer: Jae Joo,
Jae Joo Designs
jaejoodesigns.com
@jaejoo_
Architect: Baao Studio
Photography: Nick Glimenakis
nickglimenakis.com
@nickglimenakis

A FRESH START
PP. 158 & 200-211
Owners: Jose Alvarez
& Brooke Hammel
Interior Designer: Jae Joo,
Jae Joo Designs
jaejoodesigns.com
@jaejoo
Photography: Nick Glimenakis
nickglimenakis.com
@nickglimenakis

CHARM AND SOUL
PP. 212 & 214-227
Owners: Anaïs Katz
and Simon Royaux
Design: Kevin Greenberg,
Space Exploration
spaceexplorationdesign.com

@space_exploration_design
Photography: Nicole Franzen
nicolefranzen.com
@nicole_franzen

IN GOOD HANDS
PP. 228-241
Owner: Erica Sellers
Interior Designers: Erica Sellers
and Jeremy Silberberg
of Studio S II
@studio.s.ii
studiosii.com
Photography: Joseph Kramm
josephkramm.com
@joeinstakramm

AN UPPER EAST SIDE GEM
PP. 242-253
Interior Designer: Charlotte Sylvain
studiofauve.com
@studiofauve
Interior Stylist: Katalin Junek
Architect: DDG
ddgpartners.com
Photography: Nick Glimenakis
nickglimenakis.com
@nickglimenakis

Texts: Corynne W. Pless, @corynnestudio, corynnewarepless.com
Photography: Nicole Franzen, Nick Glimenakis, Joseph Kramm, Chris Mottalini, and Matthew Williams
Design: Carolina Amell, @bookpackager, amellcarolina.com
Editing: Léa Teuscher
Front cover image: Joseph Kramm

Sign up for our newsletter to read about new and forthcoming publications on art, interior design, food & travel, photography
and fashion as well as exclusive offers and events. If you have any questions or comments about the material in this book,
please do not hesitate to contact our editorial team: **art@lannoo.com**

©**Lannoo Publishers,** Belgium, 2025
D/2025/45/180 – NUR450/454
ISBN 978-94-014-3020-3
www.lannoo.com